PRAISE FOR *THE DESIRED* FLOURISH & THRIVE PROGRAMS

HERE'S WHAT OUR STUDENTS HAVE TO SAY:

"It's June 4th, and I just beat my last year's total sales for the whole year. Huge win!" — KATY BEH

"After I got divorced, I decided to be an entrepreneur and it's made me confront my greatest weaknesses. So to have success means so much more than superficial business success. My self-respect, my ability to expand myself, it's huge! And also it lets me model that to my kids: doing what I love, pushing my boundaries, hanging in there. There's nothing out there in the jewelry industry like it." — MARGARET COWHIG, MARGARET COWHIG JEWELRY

"My online sales are up 695% (yes, that is correct) from this month last year!" — MEGHAN BOEHM, MEGAN BO JEWELRY

"My design was featured on NY Live." — CAROLINE BRUCE, TWEAK BOUTIQUE

"I made more in the past six months than I did in all of last year. I've gotten over my fear of emails, and I've found my voice as a designer and feel confident being the face of my brand. I recouped $30K in lost wholesale orders. I've built a name and a brand ID that's strong enough that quality collaborators are now reaching out to me. This is my passion and having my own company and designing jewelry is my calling." — JESSICA LAWSON, DEA DIA JEWELRY

"After changing my mindset, I raised my prices between 30-50% and I continue selling without a problem!" — GISELA CLEMMENS

"My marketing is working!" — ALLISON KALLAWAY YOUNG, ALLISON KALLAWAY JEWELRY

"I've hit goals I never thought were possible!" — ALEX CAMACHO, ACID QUEEN JEWELRY

"I'm always appreciative of the support and unyielding energy that the coaches put into helping. I don't think I would have survived my first year in business without them, just on the mindset side of things. It's a great resource for anyone who's feeling the least bit insecure about what they're doing."

"I have clarity on who my Dream Client is and my website is one that I am proud of." — CANDACE STRIBLING, CANDACE STRIBLING JEWELRY

"We upped our prices in hopes of attracting our Dream Client and it has worked! We now have four fully custom engagement ring clients on the books and another two or three beginning talks. This is the part of designing that I love and am unbelievably excited!" — JEANA AND JARED RUSHTON, FOX AND THE STONE

"My sales are up 400% since last year and I landed a huge contract with TikTok." — GITTI LIDNER, CINDER CERAMICS

"I'm selling out of my collections every season." — ANDREA LI, ANDREA LI JEWELRY

"After being in business for 20+ years, I was burned out and ready to throw in the towel. My creativity had been sucked dry and I had nothing left for my family. During the year we worked together, I was able to streamline my operation and save over $18,000 a month. I finally feel joy in my business again and can bring that home to my family." — JENNIFER DAWES, JENNIFER DAWES DESIGNS

"I finally didn't have any more excuses about why I couldn't do this." — KENA TREADWAY, FEW MADE JEWELRY

"My profits grew by 65%." — JOANNE SIMMONS, THE SILVER SCULPTOR

"It's given me more confidence than I ever expected." — DENISE KUBLER, DK ORIGINALS

"I have been in business for about 35 years now. But it's really hard to say that because my business was lost before this. I really just had an expensive hobby. There were so many things I didn't know! The [Desired Brand Effect] was life-changing for me. My sales increased by 25%! I am a better business person because of Laying the Foundation." — BELINDA WICKWIRE, BELINDA WICKWIRE JEWELRY

"My social media following is up by at least 75%. It's been incredible. And I've already surpassed my entire last year's sales!" — PEGGY HOUCHIN, PEGGY HOUCHIN JEWELRY

"I've more than doubled my sales this year." — ALYSSA MINER, JAMMIN HAMMER JEWELRY

"Pretty much everything I've learned about being in business, I've learned from Flourish & Thrive." — ERIN HEYDENREICH, BETINA ROZA JEWELRY

"[The DBE] has completely changed the way I run my business." — WENDY HIVELY, CHARLIE MADISON ORIGINALS

THE DESIRED BRAND EFFECT

STAND OUT IN A
SATURATED MARKET WITH A
TIMELESS JEWELRY BRAND

Tracy Matthews

Published by Flourish & Thrive Academy via Creative Launchpad LLC
www.flourishthriveacademy.com

The information given in this book should not be treated as a substitute for legal or financial advice, and should never be used without first consulting with a financial professional to determine what may be best for your needs.

The author does not make any guarantee or other promise as to any results that may be obtained from using the content of this book. Case studies provided in this book are independent and genuine. However, they do not represent a guarantee or warranty of similar results.

Cover design by Flourish Online
Front Cover Image: Raquel Lauren Photography at RaquelLauren.com
Front Cover Jewelry: The Fox and Stone at TheFoxandStone.com
Back Cover Image: Krista Little at ShutterGoesClick.com
Back Cover Jewelry: Jennifer Dawes Designs at Dawes-Design.com
Editing by Kris Emery Editorial

ISBN (paperback): 978-1-7343228-0-4
ISBN (e-book): 978-1-7343228-1-1

This book is dedicated to my mom. You embodied the definition of fun. Your death so many years ago showed me that life was too short to not follow my dreams.

Scan here for Resources

CONTENTS

PART ONE:
CREATING DESIRE

PART TWO:
SHARING DESIRE

PART THREE: SCALING DESIRE

PART FOUR: TYING IT ALL TOGETHER

INTRODUCTION

You're a maker, a creator, an expert in your craft. Your dream is to build a profitable, sustainable jewelry business that supports the kind of lifestyle you want, giving financial stability, freedom, and a sense of accomplishment. You're on the path to creating desire for the jewelry you make as you carve out a space for your brand in the market. You know it's possible, because now more than ever consumers want to support emerging talent like yours. You've glimpsed that for yourself and now you need more people to find you and fall in love with what you create.

Maybe you've had a bit of success selling your jewelry. Maybe even a lot of success. Yet creating longevity in the market and growing a sustainable business still eludes you. Perhaps you feel like you've been building your business with a piecemeal approach or working so hard to create success that you're wondering if it's even worth it. You're not alone. Most artists, makers, and creatives struggle to create a distinct brand voice, clearly communicate their message, and develop a brand story that resonates with their Dream Clients. Even fewer manage to build on that so their business gains momentum from the effort they put in with their buyers, turning them into true fans who do the selling for them. And fewer still succeed in growing their business to a place where it continues to run smoothly without them running the day-to-day.

What if you could, though? What if you easily attracted the types of customers and collectors who became true fans and life-long brand advocates for your beautiful creative products? What if you never had to stress out through another dry spell or worry that your voice was drowning in a sea of other makers' voices?

When you can create desire for your brand, you become the only choice in the eyes of your Dream Clients. Sales and marketing become easy because you have a system for marketing that fuels the sales engine. As the sales and marketing make your revenue more predictable, you get to spend more and more time in a creative role—planning collections, designing, creating buzz for your jewelry (or products) and hanging out in that creative space you love, the reason you started in the first place. When you have people sharing desire for your brand, they're doing the hard work for you so you can focus on your next step—whether that's bringing more people in to help you or creating ease and flow to make things happen faster and better behind the scenes.

All this is possible when you understand and apply the Desired Brand Effect™ methodology, which I've created from my own experience in growing six- and seven-figure businesses over the last 25-plus years.

I'm Tracy Matthews, jewelry designer, entrepreneur, mentor, and host of the top-rated Thrive By Design podcast. As the Chief Visionary Officer of Flourish & Thrive Academy™ and Creatives Rule the World™, I help creatives and visionaries follow their dreams, make money doing what they love, and take control of their lives. I've been designing jewelry for most of my career and I'm obsessed with helping other designers like you attract your raving fans and repeat buyers who become your brand advocates so that you can supercharge your sales, online and off.

Over the past nine years, it has been my mission to help as many creatives as possible provide financial security for themselves and their families by giving them the skills they need to take their power back and grow successful jewelry businesses.

The Desired Brand Effect was the system I developed to position, grow and scale four companies across multiple industries including jewelry, education, and branding. My style is to make business-building fun, filled with ease, and aligned with who you want to be and what you want to stand for as a brand.

In this book, I am going to teach you how to expand your audience, grow your sales, and amplify your results with a simple model that you can apply no matter where you are in business. Every chapter comes complete with resources that will inspire you to apply what you're learning and stay on task. From branding and positioning to marketing and sales to systems and automation, this book will demystify the business side of running, streamlining and scaling a creative products brand.

When you create the Desired Brand Effect in your business, you'll stand out in the saturated jewelry market with a timeless brand that your customers not only remember and desire but can't wait to share with everyone they know. You're about to create, share and scale desire for a brand that eliminates the competition because you're the only choice in the eyes of your true fans! If you're ready and willing to take the first step of reading this book, I'm here to take you on that journey...

...to your Desired Brand.

CHAPTER 1

BECOMING THE CHIEF VISIONARY OFFICER OF YOUR BUSINESS

"In order to create a truly successful business, you've got to work on it, not just in it."
— MICHAEL GERBER

As the artist that you are, you did not decide to run your business to be overworked and trapped in the day-to-day. You started a jewelry business because you had a huge dream, a passion for design, and a willingness to go out on your own to make a living doing what you love, no matter the risks. You turned your talent into your vocation because you wanted to share that passion with the world and spend your time being creative. When you started, you were likely overflowing with inspiration and excitement about making beautiful products, but perhaps you didn't give much thought to the business side, or more precisely what it would *really* mean to make your way in this industry with a jewelry *brand*.

This was certainly true for me when I opened the doors to my first business as a jewelry designer over 25 years ago. I started Tracy Matthews Designs, Inc. to share my talent and make a living from my creativity. It was only later that problems began to show, and I experienced my business as disjointed and draining.

Six months in, my now-ex told me, "If you don't start making sales soon, you're going to have to go back to your retail job." No way was I going back to retail. These words lit a fire under me to succeed; I worked harder and spent many years growing a business through trial and error, struggling to figure it all out on my own. Eventually, I gained some traction and started getting recognized.

As my business grew, I realized I hadn't been thinking about how all of the independent parts of the business were connected to each other, so I kept driving forward with sales without creating systems in my business that would allow me to work less and get more out of the time I was putting in. The result? I became stuck in a pattern of feast or famine with a poorly run operation. I spun my wheels doing repeatable work, which was frustrating and uninspiring. I spent my time focusing on my weaknesses in business instead of my strengths. I saw my sales increasing, but this was overwhelming without the support systems to back them up, especially when all my efforts didn't amount to the kind of financial results I wanted. At a certain point, I had barely any time to do anything I liked or spend my weekends with my family and friends—the reason I had started the business in the first place. I was exhausted from working well into the evenings, sometimes seven days a week, and I had basically created a job for myself. This was not what I expected the life of an entrepreneur to be like. My creativity was tapped. My vision was shortsighted. I was so busy being reactive in my business that I didn't have time to focus on the aspects that I loved.

Not having a clear vision, plan or systems became a challenge down the road when I wanted to hire employees. I hadn't been thinking strategically about how to keep it all running without me and documenting the way I did everything. I'm naturally inclined to be a quick-starter who doesn't need a lot of information to get things going, and maybe you're the same, but when your objective is to grow a business, something has to change.

I'd been in business several years and had made multiple six figures when someone suggested I read Michael Gerber's book *The E-Myth: Why Most Small Businesses Don't Work and What To Do About It*. I remember sitting in my new office in NYC—a small 10 x 10 space with peeling paint on the walls and no windows that I shared with three team members after relocating from San Francisco—going through the numbers with my new accountant when he said, "Tracy, have you heard of *The E-Myth*?" Given the title, I was insulted at first at the suggestion that I needed to read it! However, when I opened the book, I was blown away. It was what my business had been missing the whole time. In *The E-Myth*, the author describes how most businesses "fail to achieve their potential because most business owners are not Entrepreneurs; they are Technicians suffering from an entrepreneurial seizure." This book made me realize how I'd been acting like a Technician and that my business was more of an expensive hobby than an enterprise that offered me freedom and financial security.

Technicians live in the present and focus on making, selling and delivering their product or service, as opposed to achieving results through people and systems, and strategizing for the future. While Technicians exist in every type of business, in the jewelry industry, this idea of doing the all the work of making your products by yourself is what I call having a Maker Mindset.

Reading that book was the moment I woke up to my own Maker Mindset and started acting like the leader of my business. I reframed my thinking around business visioning being boring and set about creating a new role for myself—the position of Chief Visionary Officer or CVO. Everything opened up in a short space of time and I was quickly able to play in my sweet spot: finding new prospects, working on design with clients, and coming up with the big picture vision. Very soon, I learned the reality that being the CVO of my company was in fact the *most* creative role I could take on in my business, and the success I was looking for followed.

The Difference Between Maker and Chief Visionary Officer

When they start out, most designers don't really think of themselves as the head of a company, and yet, it's a crucial mindset to adopt if you want to grow your business beyond being a side hustle. Before I go on, I want to stress that there's nothing wrong with making your art as a side business or designing jewelry as a hobbyist while holding down a full-time job or running another business. Those are completely valid paths for some people, and I am not disparaging them as options. However, if you're here, it is likely that you have made the decision to create, grow and sustain a jewelry brand. And to do that, you'll have to make another decision—one where you decide to step out of the role of Maker and into the shoes of Chief Visionary Officer.

Here is how we define a few of the roles you might be playing in your business as it stands.

> **Maker:** Someone who has a skill and uses it to make some sort of product or service. In this case, it would be designing or making your art.

> **Manager:** Someone who oversees and controls the flow of other people doing their job. They are responsible for manifesting the company vision and business plan.

> **CVO:** The visionary of a creative product company whose responsibilities include creative direction, designing, business planning, final decision-making, and overseeing all aspects of the business.

If you're wondering why you bought this book when I'm only going to tell you to stop making your art, let me reassure you that I will be showing you the path to a profitable jewelry business that makes you more money and gives you back more of your energy and time. In order to achieve this, you have to start thinking like a visionary leader, but believe me when I say that this allows you to be even more creative than the roles you are stuck in now.

For example, the kinds of tasks and activities you may find yourself juggling as the Maker of your business include:

- Responding to inquiries and questions from prospective customers and retailers
- Taking and fulfilling orders, including making the products and shipping them
- Negotiating with suppliers and overseeing orders of supplies
- Managing inventory
- Being present on all your marketing channels
- Creating and posting content
- Dealing with returns or complaints

Compare these with the main responsibilities of a Chief Visionary Officer of any creative product brand:

- Creative direction: designing collections, brand vision, overall creative integrity of the company
- Business planning: the entire package of your combined plans including projected growth, setting goals, financials, operations, HR, sales and marketing
- Final decision-making
- Company vision
- Driving the brand
- Leading the marketing and sales efforts

You may identify a number of day-to-day tasks in the Maker list that are familiar to you, and wonder what a lot of those in the CVO list even are. In order to start seeing yourself as the leader of a business, here are some scenarios that compare the behaviors of a business owner who is acting as a Maker side by side with the way a CVO might tackle a situation. (Please note: the extremes are for effect!)

	MAKER MINDSET	VISIONARY LEADERSHIP
CREATIVITY	reactive, piecemeal, unplanned, designs influenced by own taste, expenditure is random and also according to likes and dislikes	strategic, branded, cohesive, designs influenced by sales potential and past results, supplies are well-considered and under control
DECISIONS	emotional decision-making without regard for what is best for business	responsible, objective, rational decision-making
FINANCES	unaware, avoidant, deluded, afraid to look at the numbers in case it is as bad as feared	sharp, savvy, monitoring consistently, addressing problems head-on, looking to the long term, open to making adjustments
OPERATIONS	disorganized, unprepared, undocumented, not anticipating problems or articulating what help is needed, not hiring based on needs	organized, grounded, well-documented, supported, repeatable tasks are easily picked up by new support team members, hiring for skill and experience
STRATEGY	vague, oblivious, non-committal, hopeful	specific, aware of growth potential, future-focused, taking action on longer-term dreams
PRODUCT	retains control, does everything, fails to see the possibilities of outsourcing	outsources production, values time

Creativity

In the Maker Mindset, a designer is a Creative Reactionary who narrowly focuses on design, lacks future vision, does not have a plan and creates with blinders on. The Maker has no strategy for growth or design but rolls with the punches. They spend most of the cash coming in the door without tracking numbers or looking ahead at potential expenses. They prefer to wing it and are buoyed when they see some success but worried when there is a sales lull.

On the other hand, a designer in the CVO role acts like a Creative Visionary. This means they design collections, create branded visions, track financials, and are innovative with design and inspiration. The Visionary likely has a one-year and three-year plan for growth and design development and a five-year vision they're shooting for. They keep a solid business plan (not the 50-page kind), track the progress of the company against that plan, and make adjustments so that they are able to hit their sales projections and profit numbers.

As a designer in the Maker Mindset, our business owner is a Design Amateur. The Maker designs because *they* like something without considering all the other factors that maximize their profits on any given design. They design whatever they like because it's pretty, but end up with either low margins or pieces that aren't priced to sell. This can result in extra inventory or low sales. They keep their favorite designs in their collection because they are attached to them regardless of how well they are doing or whether they're good strategic design choices.

As a CVO, the business owner becomes a Design Maestro who designs with the end in mind. They consider how the design will affect production, costing, sales, and overall expenditure to the company. During the design phase of each new collection, they are strategic about costing, quality, and margins. They cut any designs that don't have enough profit margin based on perceived value or ease of manufacturing.

When it comes to inventory, it is no surprise that the Maker is also an

Inventory Amateur, buying what they love with little regard for how it fits into a collection because they haven't created that vision yet. As a result, they end up with boxes of random supplies stashed in overflowing cupboards for years and no clue what to do with them all. They are seduced by bright shiny objects and max out their credit cards to purchase them. When they get their supplies back to their making space, they realize they've bought too much useless stuff. Instead of returning duplicates and supplies bought in error or finding another way to reduce inventory, they throw the extra materials into a box to "deal with later."

A Visionary Leader takes charge of their supplies like an Inventory Master. They keep a close eye on inventory and its direct correlation to profitability. They save any scrap to reuse or return. In the case that they end up with extra inventory, they strategize ways to sell it off and get rid of it quickly.

Decisions

When making decisions, the Maker avoids looking at the cause and effect of their actions and is an Emotional Decision-Maker. They base decisions on emotions without looking at how it will play out financially. This often looks like labor fees getting out of hand and continually shrinking margins. They know they have to cut overhead, but do not like the idea of letting go of a team member who isn't performing because they've become a friend. Instead, they can't stay objective with their staff, which results in reducing profits or a decision to cut the more efficient team members who aren't as fun or cool to be around.

In a CVO Mindset, the business owner is an Objective Decision-Maker who considers the big picture and bases decisions on what is best for the company, even if that means making tough choices. Their point of view is objective even if the decision is counter to their feelings. If labor fees get out of hand or margins shrink, the Visionary Leader takes steps to evaluate and keep only the most efficient team members for growth.

Finances

In the Maker Mindset, the designer is Financially Frightened, afraid to look at their numbers and benchmark goals because they have a feeling that they are not making enough money. And they are correct! The Maker's attitude is "I'm an artist, not a numbers person" and they do not consider it their job to look at the financials. They might use credit to finance the business—just like they did when it was still a hobby—or they hope for a magical business partner who is going to invest in their fledgling company and run the day to day. If they are even paying attention to expenses and notice them rising, they are unable to figure out why. Instead of troubleshooting at this point, the Financially Frightened designer ignores all the warning signs and continues their spending behavior.

Our CVO designer is Financially Savvy. They look at the financials of the business consistently so they know if the business is where it should be. If sales numbers are low, they strategize to find ways to hit their goals. If sales have exceeded expectations, they revise their goals to allow for more income. They focus on profitability so they can pay themselves and their team. They use cash flow to finance their business for the long term. If margins decrease when developing a new collection, the Financially Savvy CVO does the work to figure out why. They immediately identify problems and adjust accordingly.

Operations

In a Maker Mindset, our designer is Operationally Destructive, meaning they get frazzled every time something goes unplanned. And that happens a lot. They are *completely disorganized* but they can't understand why they spend more of their day answering questions than working on or in their business. They have no solid systems, so when they hire a new intern, contractor, or employee, they are immediately frustrated when that person can't figure out how to do the job without any training. They end up letting them go because it's easier to do everything themselves.

They are clueless about how to lead a team and have a laissez-faire attitude to management. They expect people to find or figure out their own way of doing everything. They hire people they could be friends with, as opposed to hiring based on skill-set and experience.

Contrast this with the CVO who is Operationally Optimal. A leader understands that a smooth operation with solid systems is the only way to run an efficient, profitable business. They are calm and collected when they interact with their support team—either contractors or employees—because they have documented operations and created step-by-step instructions for how to do just about anything in the business. When this CVO hires a new team member, it's a breeze to train them because everything is written down and tasks are templated.

They understand the importance of being objective when managing a team. They are in charge of hiring and make decisions based on ability, skill and experience.

Strategy

The Maker is a Business Butterfly who flutters from one thing to the next without direction. They ask, "Strategy? What strategy?" They set "loose" quarterly and yearly sales, marketing and business plans, oftentimes keeping them all in their head rather than committing them to a spreadsheet or accounting software system. They are inconsistent when tracking sales as they come in. They think they are hitting their numbers until their bookkeeper tells them that the actual sales figures are way below what they thought. Instead of taking action, the Maker is paralyzed by feelings of failure.

A Maker may also prefer to only look at what is in front of them. They make all of the pieces themselves but have no real vision of where the company can or will go. They see themselves as artists, not business people or entrepreneurs, and they aren't "into" strategy. As such, they are noncommittal about the future and don't have a plan to grow, only a dream that their art will be discovered someday without proactively going after their dreams.

By comparison, having a CVO mindset means that the owner is a successful Business Strategizer. This person makes solid yearly and quarterly sales, marketing and business plans. They are revenue-focused and goal-oriented. In fact, exceeding their goals is one of the most exciting parts of being in business.

The Chief Visionary Officer of a jewelry brand does not leave anything to chance. When it comes to future success, they focus *most* of their time on the business vision, the bigger picture, future goals and dreams, and strategic planning. This type of designer is strategic about goals and wants to have a multichannel brand with retail accounts, an e-commerce branded website, and wholesale accounts. They leave nothing to chance and take concrete steps toward their dreams; the goal itself does not matter, but the act of turning vision into reality is a trait that the CVO practices again and again.

Product

As a Production Maker, the person who has a Maker Mindset cannot wrap their head around stepping away from doing everything themselves. They don't see the value in outsourcing the making of the pieces, because that's why they started a business in the first place. This is a result of not seeing the value in freeing up their time to focus on more highly leveraged activities. On top of this, hiring someone to make their products is an expense that they don't think they can afford. By not removing themselves from the process, the Production Maker actually makes far less. It's what might be termed "creating a job for yourself" instead of focusing on activities that generate revenue and grow a business. This Maker will continue to make everything, overworking and staying up late to get everything done, despite their "hourly rate" being minimal when they work out how much time they put in. In fact, they often think of themselves as hourly wage earners instead of the principle of their company who earns a salary.

The relationship between a Visionary Leader and their product creation is about being a Production Ace, as they understand the importance of taking themselves out of the production equation. They know their time is more valuable than what they can pay another production worker, manufacturer, or jeweler—someone who is not a business owner and does not want to be an entrepreneur—to do. The overarching theme here is that the Production Ace removes themselves from being the Technician. Instead they eventually hire people who can move much more quickly with no loss of quality, increasing productivity and profit margins. The Production Ace realizes that their time is better spent focused on growing the business and they consider themselves the leader of the company with a salary.

Steering My Business as a Visionary Leader

You might be wondering how I went from being in that Maker Mindset to standing in the role of Chief Visionary Officer when I started my jewelry business all the way back in the 90s. The answer is: so much mindset work! This is why mindset is a central part of Laying The Foundation and Momentum, our two core programs at Flourish & Thrive Academy. I'll give you some mindset tools in a later chapter of this book, but for now let me paint the picture of what flipping the script allowed me to do when I was a jewelry designer starting out.

I had a passion for designing jewelry and I wanted to make a living doing what I loved. In college and beyond, I often worked evenings and almost every weekend, but I didn't want that for myself anymore. I wanted time for my friends and family, to see my nieces and nephews growing up, to be a part of their lives, and I knew deeply that a business could offer the financial security and lifestyle freedom that would allow me to do this. I wanted my business to be financially abundant and to grow easily with intention and direction. I wanted to have a flexible schedule and a team that was on board with my vision to grow my brand. I wanted to be able to retire early and enjoy my life. I wanted to be happy; happy because I was the one running the show, a big-shot entrepreneur. I wanted to have a business that paid me abundantly. Honestly, I had a huge dream and I thought I would be set for life by now! However, things didn't go according to plan, because even though I had a vision, I wasn't acting like a visionary.

I started my business and experienced some growth. I took on staff and other expenses. I thought everyone would figure out how to do what was needed and my business would keep growing. However, I hadn't set up the infrastructure or shared my vision with my team. Winging it had worked for a while when I was running the business alone, but now that I had others working with me, my business dysfunction had a trickle-down effect.

I was being reactionary and not learning from my mistakes, so my business started backsliding and we started losing money. I was bombarded with questions, constantly telling my team what to do, putting out fires, and not getting why this was happening. There was a time when I didn't have any money left over after we shipped a $100,000 order and I couldn't understand why. It was frustrating to be working so hard with nothing to show for it—at least not the financial abundance I was trying to create. On top of this, my team was struggling, but I was too overwhelmed and burnt out to untangle all of the issues we were having. I felt like a failure and was stretched to my limit. Why, when the business seemed to be taking off, was it also caving in?

The answer is I wasn't stepping into the role of Chief Visionary Officer. I was stuck in the role of Manager and Maker combined. And I truly believe this experience is universal for designers setting out to grow a business.

After my accountant recommended Michael Gerber's book, everything about my approach changed. I hired consultants who taught me to think and act like a visionary. Over the years and as a result of that mindset switch, I grew a pretty awesome following. My jewelry line was sold in over 350 retail outlets across the globe. My media coverage was abundant and celebrities from Halle Berry and Charlize Theron loved my work. Not only did I grow an epic brand, but my business was providing me with the freedom, lifestyle and money I desired. Shifting my mindset was the first step to changing how I looked at my jewelry business. Your mindset is one of the key factors responsible for everything in your life: your happiness, your ability to attract success, your business outlook and just about anything else.

In order for your business to grow at the pace you want, you need to be driving the business engine forward by moving toward your goals and visions with thoughtfulness, intention and solid planning. As a creative being, your circumstances might be different to the exact path I followed, but chances are that the feelings, intensity and struggle are all the same. At any stage of business, whether you are a solo maker or have a team already, you'll run into the same roadblocks unless you set up your business in the right way. From working effectively to encouraging growth, every business needs a plan. If you spend most of your time working *in* your business instead of *on* your business, you will continue to face the same issues over and over and over again.

Shifting Your Mindset

When you shift your mindset from being a Maker to being a Visionary Leader, your business will blossom and it will set you free. Being the CVO of your business is freeing because you have space to focus on the creative aspects of it instead of being stuck in the day to day.

Awareness comes first, so it's important to start by taking stock of where you are, what roles you currently do, what aspects you love and where your best talents can be utilized in your business. Where are you spending your efforts right now? Are you a Technician who is afraid to let go of the idea that you must make every single piece yourself? Are you a Manager implementing strategy and answering questions all day, constantly putting out fires and addressing short-term issues, with no spare energy for anything else? Are you an Entrepreneur working on creative direction, business planning, and company vision? There are no judgments here. Only by being completely honest with yourself can you start to step into visionary leadership.

Once you understand how you are acting out the Maker Mindset, you have a decision to make. Will you make this mindset switch and step into the role of Chief Visionary Officer for your business? Even if you are a solo entrepreneur or one-woman show, it's important for all businesses to have someone who acts and thinks like a Chief Visionary Officer, because you must know where you're going now and in the future. As your business grows, you will have to let go of a number of the roles and activities that you've been overseeing and start delegating to Managers and Technicians, because what got you here won't get you to the next stage of your business. You will need to maximize your efficiencies and improve your systems and business path so that you don't plateau or even regress.

Shifting your mindset won't be an overnight process. You will have to work *in* your business still, as you start to work more *on* your business. The key is that you are aware of how you are behaving now and begin to take baby steps (or giant leaps!) to change. Though it is key to make this mindset switch if you want to run a profitable jewelry company, it is beyond the scope of this book to share the tools of mindset work, although this is a central part of the programs I run in the Flourish & Thrive Academy.

Instead, what I am going to share for the remainder of this book is the model that a Visionary Leader of any creative products brand at any stage can follow to create business success for themselves.

A Visionary Leader sees their business as a brand—separate from *and* led by them, sought after *and* sustainable, strategic *and* stylish, customer-focused *and* creative. A successful and profitable jewelry brand means replacing trial-and-error tactics with a tried-and-true model that gets results. If you are willing to embrace this model in your business, so much will open up, including a bigger paycheck and more freedom for you.

It's time to introduce you to that methodology: the Desired Brand Effect.

CHAPTER 2

THE DESIRED
BRAND EFFECT

"The desire to make art begins early."
— DAVID BAYLES

Nothing is more valuable than seeing someone truly enjoy a piece of jewelry that you have made for them. Even better is when that person shares it with their friends! When you see your clients' happiness, joy and amazement because of the piece you have created, it gives you a sense of purpose and accomplishment, knowing that the work you do really matters to someone and that you're creating something *desired*.

What if you could get your work in front of even more potential customers and create financial security for yourself at the same time by selling what you make, doing what you love, and having an abundance of control over your time (aka freedom)? That is exactly what I was seeking when I created the Desired Brand Effect as a methodology to use myself. When I started my first jewelry company in 1998, this model helped me get exposure, build a system of repeat sales and loyal customers, and scale my business to an annual revenue of nearly seven figures. I used this model again to build another jewelry lifestyle company that regularly brings in multiple six figures a year with few staff. I've also used this model to build a multi-seven-figure business. Then in the Flourish & Thrive Academy, I've mentored over 7500 students at the time this book was written who have used this model to grow their businesses and reach their goals. In essence, I know it works!

Born out of my experience with jewelry brands, the Desired Brand Effect methodology was designed primarily for jewelry companies, but it works for all types of businesses. I focus on jewelry makers, designers and artists in this book, because of how much you love *creating*. The Desired Brand Effect methodology allows you to spend more time in that creative space. Here's how the system works and why it's so important that your business implements this strategy and grows sustainably.

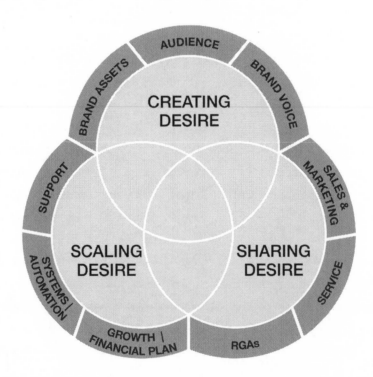

The Desired Brand Effect methodology is made of three main pillars, core areas that you will need to focus on in order to have a business that attracts people, gets them to buy your products, and allows you to do that at scale with ease. The three pillars are called:

1. Creating Desire
2. Sharing Desire
3. Scaling Desire

As you can see from the image, each pillar is broken into three focus areas that form part of the whole. You will need all of these elements for your business to grow sustainably, but where you focus at any given time depends on what you are experiencing in your business. You will cycle through the model again and again, and the process never ends. At every stage of business, you will reach a new layer of the Desired Brand Effect™ model, so whether you're just starting out or you've been in business for a while, please know there is so much you can get out of applying this methodology. The idea is to help you stop doing everything that comes your way and start thinking strategically about what is most important to your business right now. To do that, let me explain the core pillars in more depth.

For the sake of simplicity, we'll start with the Creating Desire pillar. After all, you can't serve your customers (Sharing Desire) if you don't have an audience of people wanting to buy from you (Creating Desire); you can't set up systems and automation (Scaling Desire) if you haven't got a collection to show prospective customers (Creating Desire). In that sense, most creative products brands will start here.

Creating Desire

Creating Desire is all about building your audience, attracting the right customers and becoming known for what you do. We can summarize these aspects of Creating Desire into three key elements:

- Brand assets
- Audience (prospects and existing customers)
- Brand voice and messaging

The first part of Creating Desire that you need to consider relates to all of your brand assets. Brand assets are elements of your brand that make your brand identifiable. They include your jewelry collection or the collections you're selling, packaging, logo, website, catalogs, line sheets, color schemes, fonts, and any other branding. You'll notice these are all the outward-facing visual aspects of the business; your brand is what people *see* when they come into contact with you and it's how you become known as a designer, maker, or retailer.

The second part of Creating Desire is about your audience. These are the people you sell to and those who you haven't sold to yet but who you are trying to convert into customers down the road. You might also identify these people as your Dream Clients, social media followers, email list subscribers, previous customers, and others you are trying to attract. It's a good idea to have a clearly defined vision or persona of who your Dream Client might be. We cover the topic in depth in our Flourish & Thrive Academy programs, and will touch on this concept later in this book. For the purposes of the Desired Brand Effect model, a Dream Client is the end consumer even if other retailers resell your products (aka wholesale accounts). You might also have a list of dream stores or wholesale accounts you sell to that are determined by your Dream Clients shopping at those stores.

The third piece of Creating Desire is about how you're connecting with the outside world through your core values, mission, vision, brand story, brand voice and messaging. Again, notice the outward focus. This can include your story, the words you use on your website, your product descriptions, your social media captions, and much more. There is some overlap with sales and marketing, so let's make a distinction here. You can think of the brand voice as the *personality* of your brand that underpins and sets the tone for a lot of your sales and marketing activities.

Combined, these three elements Create Desire by attracting people to what you're doing and building an audience of people who may want to buy your work. In Chapters 2, 3, 4, and 5, we will cover the concepts and actions relating to the Creating Desire segment in more depth.

Sharing Desire

Sharing Desire is all about how you're converting the audience you have built in the Creating Desire phase into actual paying customers who buy from you over and over again. This includes all of your sales and marketing activities, delivering exceptional service for the people who come into your world and focusing on revenue-generating activities. In the Desired Brand Effect model, we talk about these as:

- ◆ Sales and marketing
- ◆ Customer experience and service
- ◆ Revenue-generating activities

These are the aspects that make or break you as a brand, because Sharing Desire speaks to how you translate interest and attention into something meaningful and shareable that makes you money.

The sales and marketing pillar is about converting window shoppers into buyers. When you create an authentic brand and connect with your audience, selling becomes easy because you're focused on building relationships, creating an affinity with your brand, and coming from a place of service. You no longer have to fear selling simply because the relationship is developed through your marketing. You've already created desire, so now it's about building the know-like-trust factor and inviting the audience to become customers.

Trust is the decision phase and it starts with your ability to deliver a great customer experience at the first encounter of your brand, long before someone buys from you and long after the sale. The experience someone has with your brand before they buy is a huge factor in their decision to spend money with you. When they open their wallet and decide to buy, they're showing you that you're doing a great job. Giving new customers an excellent experience immediately after the sale continues to build that trust and gives them the confidence to come back and shop again. The most important piece is creating a reason for previous customers to connect with your brand to buy again and again. When they do, they organically refer you to their friends and you foster the cycle of repeat sales. When you have incredible service, people remember you and come back for more.

The last aspect of Sharing Desire is about revenue generation and ensuring that you are spending enough of your time doing things that bring money into the business. The key to a successful business at the core starts with your desire to spend the time it takes to build your business, grow your audience, and put the work in to hit your sales targets so your business consistently grows. That starts with spending your time on revenue-generating activities (aka RGAs).

Scaling Desire

Scaling Desire is all about taking what you've built and amplifying that with automation, systems, people, and technology. Your job here is to let these aspects do some of the heavy lifting so that time-consuming repeatable tasks aren't slowing your business down. Plus, when you have your business set up properly and you get the right support, you start to remove yourself from the day-to-day of your operation so that you can work on being the Visionary Leader or CVO who's focused on growing the business. Scaling Desire is all about using technology and automation, systems and SOPs, leaning into different types of support (like team, coaching, mentorship, and community), and creating a planning structure so that you're reaching your goals. When you do this right, everything you've done in Creating Desire and Sharing Desire multiplies. In this phase, we're looking at three core aspects:

◆ Financial and business planning
◆ Systems and automation
◆ Support, including community, mentorship and team

The first aspect of Scaling Desire includes strategic planning, setting goals for your business and understanding the numbers. If this sounds dry and boring to you because you identify as being creative or an artist, we'll help you get over that. The numbers should empower you, not intimidate you. The more you embrace a planning cadence, follow those plans, and lean into data driven metrics to create those strategic plans, the easier it will be for you to grow. This may take some training, if it doesn't come naturally to you, but anyone can learn this. It's important to track and measure what works and what doesn't so that you can focus on the aspects of your business that make a difference and support your success.

The second aspect of Scaling Desire is all about your business operations. The terms *systems*, *procedures*, and *processes* can be used interchangeably and simply mean your way of doing things. Freeing up time for you to focus on the creative direction of the business will mean handing over repeatable low-leveraged tasks to other people. Having these tasks documented in an operations manual means that anyone you hire can easily learn how your business runs, while maintaining quality and consistency. It's about making the business much easier to understand on the inside as well as supporting the customer experience on the outside.

Automation is a part of this, too. With the right technology, your systems can do some of the heavy lifting. Plus, when you take the time to set up and automate aspects of your marketing and sales, that up-front investment will pay off in faster growth and less room for error, which allows your business to grow quickly without having to work harder. A lot of people don't take the time to do this work because they already feel like they're at max capacity, but systematization can free up time on adminis- trative work, improve operational inefficiencies, and increase your sales with marketing that doesn't require you to be there every second of the day.

The final aspect of Scaling Desire is surrounding yourself with the right support. This comes in the form of a supportive community, hiring team members, educational programs, and finding a mentor or coach. On the team side, this might mean hiring employees or working with contractors, freelancers, or virtual assistants. At the start of your business, you might work with just one person remotely for five hours a week, enlisting a staff of full-time employees as you grow. It all counts! On the community side, support means connecting with business mentors, coaches, consultants, and industry peers.

The majority of businesses cannot grow successfully without outside support. We all have knowledge gaps. I hate to break it to you, but no one is fully adept at everything when it comes to running a business. That's why so many corporations have a board of advisors. If you are in this for the long haul, you may start to wonder why you keep getting the same results as you've always had. Think about it this way: what got you here won't get you there, and that means adapting to a new strategy and uplev- eling your skill set. When reaching for a new goal, you might not have the know-how to get there if you haven't done it before, or the vision to see what's not working without an external perspective. Support can come in many forms and is the entire reason that I co-founded Flourish & Thrive Academy with Robin Kramer in 2012. To this day, our programs provide that level of support to designers who want to grow and sustain a highly profitable jewelry brand.

Even though it's important for businesses at all stages to lean into Scaling Desire, when you're just starting out, it might not be the first thing you implement. However, it becomes increasingly important as you grow your sales to multiple six or seven figures. If you're in the startup phase (below six figures in annual revenue), just understanding and starting out with simple planning will change the way your business grows. Eventually, you'll need systems and SOPs to hire a team and train people if you want to get the less desirable parts of running a business off your plate. Depending on the type of jewelry you make and sell, these numbers may be relatively easy to reach. For instance, a fine jewelry designer might easily hit six figure sales their first year out of the gate, while a costume jeweler might have to sell 10 times as much to hit the same sales number. There is no exact timing on when to do this.

In fact, the key factor in deciding where to focus on any element of the Desired Brand Effect—whether that is working on your messaging, implementing better customer service practices, introducing a new marketing channel, or adding in more systems or support—will depend on the problems you're experiencing in your business. Whether you've had a recent growth spurt and you've got growing pains or your growth has slowed down, plateaued or even declined, it will be important to notice when you need to shift your focus.

Growth Zones

As you can see from the model, when everything is going right in an area you are focusing on, you'll experience some success in that aspect of your business. However, when what has been sustaining you up to a certain point is no longer working to create the same success, growth may flatten out and you might notice more problems. Let's look at some indications that you're moving in the right direction.

Consistent Sales

What happens at the intersection of Creating Desire and Sharing Desire when you're doing these aspects well? You attract traffic and build an audience, and because you have brought in the right kind of attention with your brand at the Creating Desire phase, you convert prospects into customers successfully and you keep them for the long haul. You start seeing consistency in your sales and that consistency allows you to continue finding new people to sell to. In other words, more Dream Clients encounter your brand, buy from you, and become raving fans—Sharing Desire.

Increasing Sales and Repeat Customers

At the intersection of Sharing Desire and Scaling Desire, you will see those first-time customers become repeat customers and brand advocates. When you have raving fans, you become the first choice (or the only choice), and they buy from you over and over and over again. Of course, this is of huge value to your business as your sales continue to increase. If you're doing this right, you are likely to see your profitability and sales numbers increase. You've established loyalty by providing excellent service to the people you've brought into your world, and you're generating income from a solid customer base who shares everything you design with their network. It becomes an organic referral process.

Profitability, Reach, and Impact

More important than just your sales or overall revenue numbers is profitability. You know that when you've got Scaling Desire and Creating Desire dialed in, you'll experience higher profit margins and more ease and flow. Your business reaches more of your Dream Clients, and your brand has more influence and impact. Not only might you reach more customers but also more influential customers. Here's where you see a broadening of your audience. You're able to spend more of your energy on setting the creative direction of the business, which entices the caliber of clientele that you've dreamed of having.

Together, when you're doing everything right, you'll gain financial security and freedom doing what you love. You'll experience more freedom with your time from setting your own schedule or leaning into the more visionary or creative aspect of your business. You'll also see the risks have high rewards when you feel a huge sense of purpose or accomplishment because you are making an impact on others. In other words, you're creating a legacy with your brand and your art. When all three of these core pillars of the model come together—Creating Desire, Sharing Desire and Scaling Desire—you become a role model for the people around you and have full control over your outcomes.

Plateaus

You know what's coming next, right? What happens when you aren't doing so well and implementing these important activities in your business? This is great, too, because a plateau signals that things need to change, and you can now identify what that is. It might not feel great at the time, of course, because you may find yourself frustrated and struggling or even wanting to give it all up. However, as I mentioned in the previous chapter, awareness is the first step to taking important steps toward improvement. Let's take a look at where you might be getting stuck.

Slow or Rollercoaster Sales

The surest sign that you need to lean into the Desired Brand Effect model via the intersection of Creating Desire and Sharing Desire is the dreaded feast or famine cycle (aka slow or rollercoaster sales). If you're not doing this well, you might see sales increase for a while, but then drying up for a period. This rollercoaster sales situation makes it hard to build a business. Alternatively, you might never see a sales boom. Your numbers might be consistent, but they're consistently low, which is not the definition of consistent sales you're looking for.

Growth Plateau

If you get stuck in a growth plateau, this is a crystal clear sign that you need to lean into Sharing Desire and Scaling Desire. You might be working a lot harder for less money or feel like you're spinning your wheels and not making progress. You're likely doing "all the things" but your business isn't growing. I call this growth plateau because it's characterized by overwhelm, stress, dissatisfaction, and burnout. I liken it to stage fright, where people are in the spotlight but they can't see what's going on so they freeze up. They're trying to grow their business by working harder and harder, but they're exhausted and nothing's changing. In fact, the harder they work, the harder it becomes to get out of or remove themselves from their situation.

Brand Disconnect and Sales Decline

From time to time, I encounter business owners who get stuck in the worst plateau of all between the intersection of Scaling Desire and Creating Desire. Typically what ends up happening is the market changes or the founder loses focus and sales decline because there is a disconnect with the original vision for the company. A good example of this is when a designer goes in a direction that is completely disconnected from their signature style or what they're known for. Occasionally, it might work. However, if it doesn't resonate with their customer base, their sales start to decline because of a brand disconnect. Another example might look like trying to speak to people who aren't your ideal customers, i.e. trying to reach a younger audience when your jewelry speaks to women in their fifties and sixties. A brand disconnect affects customer attraction, sales, and profit margins.

The Model that Grows With Your Business

Now that you're familiar with the Desired Brand Effect methodology, let me tell you the key to all of this. This is not a one-and-done activity. Applying this model and seeing it result in the growth you desire never ends. The Desired Brand Effect works at every level of business and will continue working each time you evolve through new milestones and reach new heights in your business.

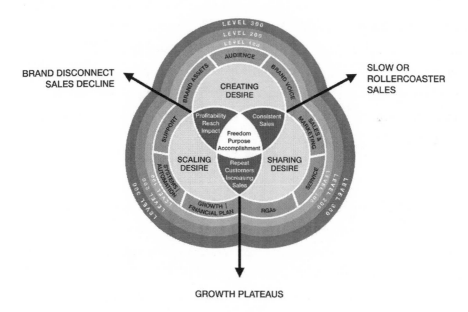

GROWTH PLATEAUS

Think of this like courses in school: you have a 100 level, a 200 level, a 300 level and a 400 level. Each level is a gateway to the next. For instance, if you'd like to become a doctor, you have to understand basic biology, then more advanced biology and anatomy, and eventually take pre-med until you apply for medical school and so on. The growth within the model never stops, and you can use this at every stage of business to identify problems in your business and overcome them with ease.

The level 100 phase lays the foundation and creates a baseline for growth. Brands at the 100 level might be just starting out in business or have been trying to grow their business for a while but haven't gained the necessary traction that building a foundation creates. Remember that Maker mindset we spoke about earlier? This is where you start to transition from Maker to CVO by building a strong business and marketing platform. In this phase, you're learning how to do this for the first time, to experience growth and financial success in your business.

At level 200, you're building a growing brand. This level is characterized by expanding on what you're already doing really well and leaning into areas of opportunity. You're likely gaining traction in this stage because you've dialed in your brand assets and brand voice. You are consistent at marketing, attracting a consistent flow of customers, and scaling your sales beyond what you can handle producing on your own. You might consider hiring an assistant or finding help with your marketing or production. You're starting to develop your systems and you utilize technology that allows you to automate aspects of your business for growth.

When you reach level 300, you're in the optimization phase, leaning into more advanced marketing strategies that require you to innovate and update your way of running a business. Even though at one point you had it nailed, here's your opportunity to refine your Dream Client avatar, update your website copy, and clarify your brand voice and messaging because, as we know, these aren't one-and-done activities. You will always revisit your core marketing and messaging, how you're attracting new customers and repeat sales, and how you're optimizing your business plan and operation. No matter the size of your company, you will always be Creating Desire, Sharing Desire and Scaling Desire, and refining it all for the evolution of your business.

At the 400 level and beyond, this is where testing and optimization becomes an important part of your long-term growth. You might expand into new sales channels, have an entire team of people helping out with all areas of your business, and set bigger goals because you're evolving as the Chief Visionary Officer of your company. When you're completely in flow, you begin to focus on the most leveraged parts of your business and delegate the parts that you don't enjoy. In this phase, you might seek out leadership training, lean into optimizing your sales funnels and marketing channels, and focus on landing more important key accounts or customers. Here is where you utilize more advanced strategies in every aspect of the Desired Brand Effect model. You'll keep expanding as there's no limit to your growth.

Freedom, Purpose, and Accomplishment

Over the years that I've worked with thousands of jewelry and creative entrepreneurs, I have found that we are all looking for the same three things when we decide to create and grow a business. Underneath it all, we want to know that we are financially secure, that the work we do matters, and that we are free to make our own choices. This is what the Desired Brand Effect seeks to help you achieve and why those core principles of freedom, purpose, and accomplishment are at the center of the model.

The purpose of the Desired Brand Effect book and all the work we do at Flourish & Thrive Academy is to support you to make this a reality. What lies behind the desire to have a lifestyle of freedom, a sense of accomplishment in your work, and the financial security to do it all is different for everyone. Some people are building a legacy, others wish to travel, many want to provide the kind of life for their children that they never had growing up. Whatever it looks like for you, always remember this is why you are building your business, especially on those inevitable difficult days that we all have. By following the Desired Brand Effect methodology, you are putting a lifestyle of freedom, meaning, and security at the center of all you do.

PART ONE:

CREATING DESIRE

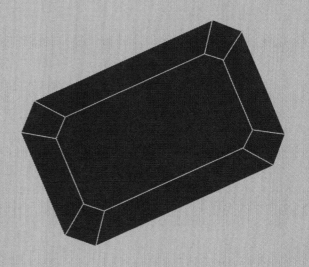

CHAPTER 3

YOUR BRAND ASSETS

"Branding is the process of creating, shaping, and influencing the desired perception you want in the marketplace."
— RE PEREZ, BRANDING FOR THE PEOPLE

When you look at any successful artist, their style is often easily identifiable throughout their career. For instance, in Claude Monet's early work from the 1870s, he had a quintessential Impressionist style with short brush strokes. Later, his work shows a major deviation in subject matter and color choice toward light pastels. Yet despite these differences, his arc as an artist is consistent throughout his lifetime. His palette changed, landscapes varied, but his essence, style, personality, and tone still shine through. This is what we mean when we talk about creating an identifiable signature style as an artist; the same is true when you create your brand.

Building a brand is important because it is what sets you apart from all the other jewelry and product businesses out there. It is the difference between an ad hoc random approach to the visual appearance of your business and a consistent look and feel that conveys all that you stand for.

A brand should be recognizable, memorable, and take your customers and true fans along with you as your business evolves.

When creating a Desired Brand, you'll need to know not only what you stand for but how you convey that to your audience. Here's why: jewelry isn't a product that your customers "need"—it is something they want, especially if you can create a pent up demand for your unique signature style. I would urge you to take branding seriously, because what your pieces can do for people is more important than you may think. Your jewelry may give them confidence to land their dream job, or hold deep memories of a lost loved one, or even be the lucky charm that attracts the love of their life. Jewelry holds deep meaning for the wearer when you understand the key motivators and reasons people buy. Never forget that your talent brings joy and amazement into people's lives—in other words, jewelry that creates the Desired Brand Effect holds a meaningful place in your customers' heart.

In this chapter, we'll cover creating a Desired Brand and the elements you need to have in place to make your business reflect who you are when you're communicating and promoting to your audience.

Definition of a Brand

When you think of your Desired Brand, it can include everything that visually represents your business. This starts with the collections you design and the products you sell as well as your website, packaging, brand assets that you use to market your work (such as catalogs, line sheets, photography, postcards, etc), branding (logo, colors, fonts, etc), and anything else that paints the picture of what you stand for as a designer or maker. You'll also need to think about how pricing communicates the perceived value of the jewelry you're selling. If you get it right, your jewelry becomes immediately identifiable, and these visual aspects will spark desire in your Dream Clients.

As you might imagine, sometimes it's difficult to put a finger on what defines your brand. After all, those concepts of tone, essence, personality and style are all rather subjective at first glance. Creating a cohesive collection is therefore an absolutely crucial place to start working on this in a concrete way.

Creating Cohesive Collections that Sell

A collection is an assortment of items where the pieces all work together to tell a story. They might be connected through a design element, a color story, or even a proprietary technique. Eventually, a signature style emerges via a common thread that is clearly evident throughout the entire collection. Designing a cohesive collection is not only practical, but also essential to communicating what your brand is all about, and building lifelong customers and raving fans. Collections that sell are merchandised and thoughtfully created with an understanding of how each piece serves a purpose to create more desire and demand. When you find your signature style and voice as a designer or maker, and apply these concepts consistently, you have the makings not just of a brand, but a Desired Brand that people recognize, know, like, trust, buy, share and love.

In order to weave a consistent theme throughout your designs and create a collection that sells, you'll need to:

- ◆ Identify a design genre
- ◆ Pinpoint your design approach
- ◆ Create a signature style

Let's take a look at each of these aspects.

Design Genres

When I was growing my first jewelry business, there were a lot of things that I did right from the get-go. Since I had a career in fashion and merchandising in retail before selling to retail stores, I understood that in order to sell a collection, I needed to have a look and a genre. So I launched my first demi-fine collection made of silver and semi-precious stones right out of the gate. However, several years into my career, I took a detour. The market had shifted from dainty, personal jewelry to fast fashion, so I wanted to play around with designing pieces in a lower price point with a bolder look. That was my short lived foray into creating a cheap and cheerful brass fashion brand. Up to that point, I had been known as the go-to brand for dainty, colorful, layering pieces, so it was no surprise (in hindsight) that my customers didn't get why I was suddenly selling brass. Needless to say, my sales suffered as a result and I had what I now call a business backslide.

Save yourself from making the same mistake and identify the genre of product that is best suited to your Desired Brand. Committing to a genre won't pigeon-hole you for life. However, the clearer you are about your artistic zone of genius, the easier it will be to evolve over time.

Your jewelry genre matters because it helps you position your brand clearly and helps your potential customers, retailers, and partners understand where you fit. If you're a newer designer or maker, I know the temptation might be to try to capture everyone by doing a little bit of everything, but it makes sense to be more specific. Typically, someone purchasing a luxury item from Mizuki or Ippolita is not the same customer who buys fast fashion collections from H&M. Likewise, someone who loves Impressionist art may not be the kind of person who likes Neoclassical art and so on. These examples illustrate how potential customers can instantly recognize when they have found what they're looking for.

Choosing a genre is about avoiding client confusion and positioning your brand in a space. If you try to do too many things at once, you'll confuse your customers or potential clients, leading to a loss of sales. Just know that there's a market for all genres.

Here are examples of the many genres in the jewelry industry:

- Ultra-fine or fine jewelry
- Demi-fine jewelry
- Fashion and costume
- Art jewelry
- Vintage, up-cycled, and heirloom redesign

Another way we could break down the genres would be to consider how the pieces are made:

- Handmade
- CAD-designed
- Hand carved and cast
- Mass-produced
- Custom or bespoke

As you're picking your genre and your lane, keep in mind there are many ways to be successful. Think about the materials you're using, the investment to develop the collection, and other costs associated with the genre you fall into.

For instance, handmade jewelry in sterling silver has been going strong for decades now, partially because the price of more precious metals like gold and platinum might be cost-prohibitive for emerging brands without investment capital. It might also be easier to get a business off the ground in more affordable materials. A GIA grad might immediately lean into fine jewelry and materials with an elevated luxe fine jewelry collection because they want to target the top-tier of society who can invest thousands into one piece for their collection. A graduate of a fashion school might immediately know that they want to design for the masses and lean into creating *avant-garde* fashion pieces. A side-hustler or self-taught hobbyist transitioning into a full-time business, however, might have learned how to make jewelry from a local jewelry supply store, so starting in a lower tier costume jewelry genre works.

Design Approach

As a maker or designer, your design approach is how you merchandise your body of work (or "line"). Merchandising is just the way you predict trends, assort your products to tell a story, and determine the price range of that assortment. You can merchandise your collection in several ways, but staying consistent in your design approach guides your creative process and helps you sell more of your beautiful jewelry because your audience knows what to expect from you.

Let's take a look at some options:

Collection designers love creating assortments of items that merchandise and work well together. For instance, you design necklaces, earrings, bracelets, and rings as a cohesive group that can be worn as separates or coordinated together. To create that cohesion, you might focus on the materials you use, your proprietary technique, special finishes, stone choices or repetitive design elements that run throughout the different pieces. There are endless examples of collection designers in the jewelry industry, including well-known brands Jennifer Dawes, Dana Kellin and Melissa Joy Manning.

Item designers create pieces that stand alone. Item-driven designers will develop one style or concept and delve deep into an array of colors, sizes, and materials for that style. The great thing about designing items? When your item is a winner, you can sell a lot of volume. Item designer examples include brands like Chan Luu and viv&ingrid whose favorite beaded hoop is still a bestseller after two decades!

One-of-a-kind designers enjoy coming up with new ideas all the time, while still creating a signature style in their designs. Depending on your genre, this kind of product should be sold at a semi-premium to premium price point due to the time it takes and expense of setting up a new model every time you make a new piece. In my second jewelry company, I chose to work at a higher price point when designing bespoke commissioned pieces in my design aesthetic so the perceived value was easily communicated. Other examples of one-of-a-kind designers are Alex Camacho of Acid Queen Jewelry, Jamie Joseph, and Lorraine West.

As you develop your design approach, consider how you want to work. Most successful Desired Brands focus on one modality, but there are always exceptions to the rule. For example, fine jewelry collection designer Jennifer Dawes also offers one-of-a-kind custom engagement rings; item designer viv&ingrid also designs capsule collections that they drop every season; collection designer Twyla Dill also drops one-of-a-kind collections a few times a year; and Lorraine West sells everyday items like her palette earrings and also has a successful one-of-a-kind fine jewelry company. You can combine design approaches in many different ways as long as the designs merchandise well together.

Signature Style

Your signature style is your design point of view that makes your pieces unique, identifiable, and unforgettable. It's your way of threading a concept throughout a particular collection and your entire line. It's the technique that you've become known for, like the intricate wire-wrapping of Dana Kellin, the dainty, gothic floral elements of Cathy Waterman, or the bold, lightweight architectural designs of Meghan Patrice Riley.

Developing a signature style takes practice, focus, and a clear vision of who you are as an artist (and who you are not). Once someone sees your work and recognizes the signature style as yours, your brand awareness amplifies. People recognize your designs when they see them just through your work alone. As an artist and creator, your signature style will evolve as you grow so don't feel trapped by developing your look and feel. When you do this right, your customers come along with you on your brand's Buyer Journey and become what Kevin Kelly calls True Fans (aka brand advocates) who buy from you every season.

For many designers, the signature style is so well integrated into their design that it seems effortless from piece to piece, collection to collection. Yet a signature style takes time to develop and is an important part of your creative process. Below are some real examples of students who have been through our Flourish & Thrive Academy programs. Take a look at these and compare their styles.

Nicole Gariepy of Fantasea Jewelry has a signature style inspired by the ocean and the beauty of the Caribbean. Core themes in her designs include swirling motifs, sea life, watery stone colors, and sterling silver with gold accents. You'll also find dragonflies, birds and flora local to her home base of St Croix depicted in her work. When you look at her designs, you can see how her location and its beautiful habitat inspires and energizes her creativity.

Jennifer Dawes is one of the leaders in sustainable fine jewelry design with a point of view. She is committed to magical design and responsibly sourced materials. Each piece combines her love of ancient civilizations, modern culture, and natural design elements. You see signature elements in her design process in the types of stones and diamonds she uses, the textures included in her work, and the proprietary techniques that have made her a leader in the alternative bridal industry.

While spending time in Turkey, Twyla Dill discovered the diminishing art of hand crocheted lace. When she returned from Turkey, she wanted a way to combine this technique into the type of jewelry she loved to wear. Twyla's signature style combines geometric shapes and modern design with her signature crocheted lace technique added on most pieces in her collections and one-of-a-kind drops.

There is no right or wrong way to go about design, but all Desired Brands have an evident style. Their consistent design point of view allows them to stand out and be recognized within the industry, rather than getting lost in the shuffle of derivative design. If you want to become a Desired Brand, you will need to develop your style so that it brings in something fresh, new and different.

Start thinking about your signature style now by reflecting on some of the brands in your jewelry niche and answering these questions:

- What elements do your favorite designers use to tie a collection together?
- What techniques and methods do they use to create their collections?
- What is it about their pieces that makes them memorable for you?
- Do they ever design anything that seems disconnected or out of place?

Answering these questions about other designers as well as your own work will help you to connect the dots between your designs and articulate that signature style that you're threading through your collections.

Merchandising

Creating a cohesive collection that sells should become second nature if you want to grow a successful jewelry brand. There are many ways to merchandise your product so that it sells. For example, you can design new collections every season and still have a solid bestselling item collection that is a staple of your brand. You might sell fine jewelry collections and also offer custom commissions for a premium price point. You might consider adding one-of-a-kind collectors' pieces to your collections every once in a while. You might also want to incorporate other products into your collection, such as lifestyle goods, fine art prints, or even soft goods like scarves. However you go about it, your approach must be cohesive and make sense to your customers and prospects.

Creating collections that sell require you to consider three elements from a merchandising standpoint: the theme of the collection, the individual components, and the assortment of styles. To highlight this, let me share a story from my own experience.

When I started out as a jewelry designer in the late 90s, I had my heart set on selling in one store in particular, Metier in San Francisco. Metier was hard to get into, so I was thrilled when the owner asked to take a look at my collection. I was even more thrilled when she loved it and placed an order. When I called a month later to check in on how things were going, she asked me to come back and show her some new pieces. She placed another big order that day and then gave me some advice that changed my whole outlook.

"Tracy, your collection is awesome and it's selling really well, but it's pretty dainty. I think it would sell even better if you had a range of styles that were a little bolder in addition to your signature dainty look."

She explained that statement pieces usually grab people's attention and get them looking at the jewelry—even if those aren't the pieces the customer ends up buying.

Once I took the store owner's advice, my sales at her store spiked and her reorders became more frequent. The moral of this story is we must look at design through the lens of how our customer buys, with each piece in a collection fitting the theme, each component being well-thought-out and the collection having a variety of styles that both draw the customer to look at the products and get them buying.

Theme

As with your design approach, design genre, and signature style, if your collection is confusing or feels scattered, it's hard for your prospects and customers to know what they should buy. And a confused customer won't buy anything, which is why it's helpful to have a theme.

The theme of an individual collection is closely related to your signature style in that it includes the design elements, techniques, style, and common idea or feeling that ties the collection together. This can be anything from a stone choice, to your design aesthetic, to your philosophy on design. It can also be tied to your influence and the techniques you use. For instance, if you design nature-inspired jewelry, you might design a collection that has a floral theme, another collection that revolves around a leaf motif, and another collection that represents bugs and insects. All of these themes are recognizable as yours even though the themes of each collection vary.

When I first started designing, the look and style of my collection was all over the place. I was testing out a lot of different types of designs, because I have eclectic jewelry taste myself. When I started seriously selling my work to stores and private customers, I realized that I sold a lot more jewelry when my collection told a story around focused themes. Since I was deeply inspired by my travels to India and my yoga practice, my Devi collection was formed. My love of nature and the sea became the muse for my "naturals" collection. Unique color combinations infused in all of my collections and were sprinkled throughout all of my designs.

Pillars of a Collection

The components or *pillars* of an individual collection are the items that make up the whole. There are three key types of items in collections that sell: statement items, gateway items, and upsell or add-on items. Here's what each of those do for you and for the customer:

Statement items are the items that draw a buyer's eye into the display, the pieces that get featured in editorial spreads, or the images that make people click through to the website. These pieces are typically enticing and larger in scale, often hitting the top price point of your range. That being said, those statement pieces may not be the bestsellers that every customer is going to buy.

Gateway items are your bestsellers, the more accessible pieces that get the customer to make their first purchase. The gateway items in your collection are typically in the middle price point range and scale comparatively to your statement and upsell pieces. They are also the pieces that attract returning or repeat customers' sales.

Upsell or add-on items are designed to match statement and gateway pieces, just on a smaller scale and at a lower entry-level price point for your brand. They are designed to build the sale or increase the average order value of a purchase. Upsell or add-on items are great additions to a collection for wholesale orders, in-person show sales, and online sales. They complement and merchandise well with other items that a customer wants to buy and can be worn alone or as a set. They might be considered giftable items since they typically are in the lower price range of your brand.

Every collection is made up of some of each of these components, almost like a merchandising formula. However, the exact number of each always depends on how the collection looks when it's displayed online and in person, because merchandising is about what sells. If you're just getting started with this concept, you can divide your collection into thirds, with one third being statement items, one third being gateway items, and one third being upsell or add on items.

Assortment of Styles

Cohesive collections typically have a minimum of 12 styles and up to 36 styles per collection. Each collection should revolve around a specific theme that is tied to a season or a group. How many collections you design per season depends on a variety of factors, including customer base, volume, and historical experience.

When I was selling my jewelry to retail stores and doing trade shows, I would release several collections every season for Spring, Summer, Fall, and Holiday. Each season might have one or two new collections and a carry over of my bestselling pieces or collections from previous seasons.

There are two mistakes that many seasoned and new designers make in their evolutionary process: expanding too quickly and doubling down too much on bestsellers in a way that becomes overwhelming. Expanding your collections too much or too fast can have a devastating effect on sales and profitability. The reverse can also be true—if you have a few bestsellers and nothing to merchandise with them, you might potentially underwhelm your buyers. In either case, both have the same effect—the risk of confusing your customers and losing the sale.

When you master the process of cohesive collection development and merchandising, create brand assets to match, and marry that with a solid pricing strategy, sales come easily.

Brand Assets

Now that we have looked at the actual products you're selling, you'll be able to offer them in a way that makes people want to buy more of your products. Brand assets are the tools that help you create desire and demand for your jewelry—in fact, packaging can be the thing that actually sells your product in certain cases. In other words, brand assets are the pieces of intellectual property that you use for promotional purposes.

Your brand assets go much further than just the pieces you design or the branding choices you make. They evoke emotion, build brand recognition, and become integral to marketing and selling your work. Great brand assets are the focal point of your brand presence. Some of the most important ones are your website, your packaging, and your promotional materials.

Website

These days, it's mandatory to have a standalone website if you want to be considered a serious designer or maker. Your website acts as a modern-day business card that creates legitimacy for you and your business. It builds a trustworthy connection with your audience and should be viewed as a tool for direct-to-consumer sales, designed to convert by moving people through your sales process.

While selling on Etsy or on Amazon Handmade are legitimate secondary sales channels, they are not a substitute for having your own website. For one, you do not have control over your relationship with the customer and can't market to those people after they buy from you. Those platforms also come with the risk that they can close your account at a moment's notice and your business will be gone overnight.

At Flourish & Thrive Academy, Shopify is our favorite platform because the plug-and-play templates make it easy to use and it has robust e-commerce functionality. It can grow along with you and is suitable for everyone, from creators who are just starting out to brands that are making tens of thousands per week. You can also set up a duplicate shop or page for your wholesalers. (If you'd like to test out Shopify, go to FlourishThriveAcademy.com/Shopify to grab a special free trial that we negotiated for you.)

Your website is such a huge topic that we can't go into all the details of what you need to know about creating a website that converts in this book. If you are starting from scratch, check out the resources section for the website training I made for you. Or head to DesiredBrandEffect.com/resources for additional resources for your website.

Packaging

Beautiful packaging is an amazing way of Creating Desire when designed in alignment with your visual brand story. In the days where physical products were only sold in stores, packaging was often something that amplified the perceived value of an item.

Today, when consumers share unboxing experiences across social media platforms, it helps validate your brand, attract new customers, and create social proof. When someone unboxes your products publicly, or even privately, you build trust with their friends, family, and followers. These types of posts are great tools as a "look-what-I-just-bought" form of user-generated content and can also be used by your brand in ads.

Photography

Photography is one of the key marketing assets for your jewelry brand. The types of photography you use tell your brand story and call out your Dream Clients in a very specific way. There are several types of photographs every designer needs. Product shots for line sheets, press or media hits, and your website's shopping section should be on a clean white or transparent background. Stylized shots and model shots are wonderful for your website home page, your blog, Instagram, Facebook, and Pinterest. Stylized and model shots are a key part of communicating your story and evoking brand emotion visually. When you've done a great job with your photography, your customers and prospects will see themselves in your brand.

Business Cards and Postcards

There's some debate about the effectiveness of "paper" assets, yet business cards, postcards, and note cards are valuable tools that you can hand out in real life exchanges, or drop in the mail to remind buyers of your brand or thank them for their purchase. Digital printing platforms allow you to use multiple different images on a small run of postcards and business cards. It's a great way to highlight your stylized photography and show more than one piece at a time.

Line Sheets, Lookbooks, and Retail Catalogs

Every designer needs a visual representation of their jewelry in a digital and/or print format. Line sheets, retail catalogs and lookbooks all serve a similar purpose in creating your Desired Brand.

A line sheet is typically used for wholesale and represents the collections you have available for wholesale purchases. The most important part about a good line sheet is that it's a way for a buyer to browse the collection and be able to make a decision based on photos if they want to carry your line or not. Ideally, your primary photos are shot on white backgrounds while secondary stylized shots (if needed) represent the size and scale of the product. Your line sheets should include wholesale pricing information, order minimums, terms and conditions for ordering, company information and contact details, an order form or instructions on how to order, and an artist bio.

A lookbook is similar to a line sheet except that it's more of a stylized brochure of a current season's collection that shows the lifestyle of your brand. Typically, lookbooks feature lifestyle and model shots and tell the story of your brand.

A retail catalog is a hybrid of both a line sheet and a lookbook that is sent to the general public. It's not mandatory, but a nice-to-have asset for your brand advocates and raving fans to browse through and order from. A catalog combines both lifestyle and white background shots of the pieces you have available to sell at retail pricing.

Press Kit

A press kit or media kit is a pre-packaged collection of promotional or marketing materials that is used to get exposure for your brand. They can be in print and digital format on your website and typically contain infor-mation for press, retail stores, and customers. The purpose is to provide detailed information about the company, including any media features or celebrity placements, new collection announcements, strategic part-nerships or collaborations, and celebrity or influencer placements. Press kits are important brand assets that build trust and credibility with your prospects, customers, and wholesale buyers. Also, they help you get more exposure, land new accounts, and create trust via social proof.

Whether you're a seasoned designer or a newbie, your brand will always be evolving. As you evolve, so do your brand assets and collections. Remember, implementing these stages of the Desired Brand Effect is an ongoing and fluid process. You can always go deeper to uncover the best ways of honing your brand for you and your customers. In our signature program, Laying the Foundation, we do a deep dive into collection devel-opment, pricing, and brand asset concepts. If you're stuck in a rut with your branding right now and need some personalized attention, we'd love to help you grow your business the right way. For more information, head over to FlourishThriveAcademy.com/LTF

Other Visual Branding Elements

If your brand wore an outfit, what would it choose to put on? Would it have beautiful designer shoes and luxury handbags? Would it get dressed up and styled everyday in the latest Veronica Beard or would it be more comfortable in Gap pajamas? Would it exist in this century or live in a futuristic society on Mars?

The point of asking is to get you thinking about the visuals and colors for your brand. Knowing what resonates with your Dream Client can help, and in the next chapter, I'll demonstrate the kind of depth you need to go into with knowing who your customers are. For now, know that your Dream Clients are your Dream Clients because you have common likes and dislikes, so make sure you keep this aligned for your brand and you aren't trying to please everyone.

A logo is the visual "mark" of your brand in a small graphic element. Don't underestimate the power of a really great logo that ties your brand together. Creating a great logo can serve many purposes from being the maker's mark on your designs to the key identifier on your website. You'll use it on packaging, marketing emails, ads, social media, and all the other assets you use to promote your brand. Do yourself a favor and hire a professional designer to create your logo. Unless graphic design is your career, you'll save yourself a lot of pain. You're welcome!

Choosing your brand's fonts and colors is a fun part of communicating what your brand is all about. Colors evoke emotions, moods, and feelings. Are you going for a luxurious look, a fun and playful vibe, or a natural and sustainable feel? The colors you choose will create that branded experience. Remember, there are over 50 shades of grey to choose from, so choose wisely.

Pricing Your Products

Pricing is one of the most confusing and controversial subjects to nail down because there is no right or wrong way to price your jewelry. The reason it's important to get this right is twofold: first, your pricing is a huge contributor to the perceived value of your products and an important part of the buying decision; second, you need to price so that you have proper wholesale and retail margins to keep your business (and each product) profitable.

It would solve a lot of problems if there was a one-size-fits-all pricing formula, but the truth is there is no cookie-cutter method for pricing your pieces.

While you might get caught up in fears about charging too much or raising your prices, charging too little can do as much or more damage as overpricing your jewelry. Case in point, we had a designer in our community who was struggling to sell a beautiful ring she designed. She kept lowering the price on the ring expecting it to sell and every time she lowered the price, nothing happened. So with our encouragement, she decided to double the price of the ring over the regular retail price and it sold within 15 minutes. It might sound counterintuitive, but that just shows how complex this topic can be and why you need a pricing strategy that works for your brand.

Perceived Value

When considering pricing, perceived value is very important. Perceived value goes beyond just the "price" of your jewelry, perceived value is just the perception of desirability of your products in the customers' eye. Your customers' perception of the value you deliver can change, so it's your job to communicate that value clearly through your brand story, product, pricing, and messaging so that price resistance becomes a non-issue.

To drive this point home, take a look at this study done by Tim Calkins and the Kellogg School of Management that was featured in my friend Re

Perez's book: *Your Brand Should Be Gay Even if You're Not*. During a focus group, he asked a group of students what they'd pay for a pair of 18K gold earrings. The average answer from the student was $550. He asked a different group of students the same question but pre-framed it by telling them the earrings were from the iconic brand, Tiffany and Co. This time the average answer was in the ballpark of $871. He asked a third group the same question, this time telling the group the earrings were from Walmart. Guess what the group valued the earrings at? This time $87.

Perceived value is more heavily influenced by brand positioning and packaging than by the object that's actually being sold. That's why brand positioning from product and packaging all the way through a brand story increases perceived value. If you don't communicate this well, you might be stuck competing on price (instead of positioning your brand like Tiffany or a successful, independent designer).

As a brand, you must know who you are, who you sell to, and how to package that to your audience. You know you've designed a cohesive collection when you are communicating what you stand for as a designer and this results in a strong market position with Dream Clients lining up to buy from you every season.

Here's an example of how I've successfully communicated the value of jewelry in the past. One of my clients asked me to design a ring for him—a simple hammered men's wedding band. He sent me an inspiration board with images from my site and other platforms like Etsy. There was one hammered band that he could have easily purchased on Etsy for $300. However, he was willing to pay my price at the time of $1200 knowing the ring would be one-of-a-kind and made just for him. You may wonder why he didn't go ahead and buy the similar design that he had seen on Etsy and provided as style inspiration, even though it was a quarter of the price. The answer is perceived value. Customers pay a premium for one-to-one attention and unique-to-them pieces.

Another example of perceived value is where customers are willing to pay a premium for an iconic brand, such as Tiffany & Co. Their iconic Heart Tag silver bracelet is priced at $310, easily double and maybe even triple the price of similar bracelets from other jewelers or "knock-off" brands. Again, this is perceived value in play. Customers value the prestige and iconic name of this brand and love owning something from Tiffany & Co.

Creating strong perceived value will improve your ability to charge the right price for your designs, create intense desire for your brand, and attract repeat customers. It can even make selling painless and fun. This value must come through in your visual branding, brand story, messaging, and communication. Let's say you're speaking to a client for the first time about a custom engagement ring. When discussing the design process, you might emphasize the time involved, the quality of the materials, the individualized product, the personalized attention you provide, the exquisite design, and the experience you give. When you do this right, your pricing and perceived value override any comparison to a mass-produced, lower-priced piece.

Remember, people buy jewelry not because they need it, but because they *desire* it, which means jewelry is often a deeply emotional purchase for the buyer.

For example:

- An engagement ring and wedding band represent the love a couple shares.
- Jewelry purchased on a vacation brings back memories of that once-in-a-lifetime trip.
- Jewelry with gemstones might evoke the energy of the stone or a healing experience.
- Jewelry designed from family heirlooms captures the memories of a loved one.

Customers will also pay more for something that aligns with their values of responsibility, uniqueness, quality, sustainability, love, and so on. Make sure you can communicate the emotion around what you do and thread it through your website, branding, copy, content, product descriptions, and all forms of marketing.

Pricing Formula

Since pricing is such a complex topic, it's beyond the scope of this book to look at it in detail here. Below is a basic formula to simplify pricing for creative products, but keep in mind that there are variations depending on your business and the type of product you are selling.

First, know your numbers:

- ◆ Cost of materials per item
- ◆ Cost of labor to make each item
- ◆ Overhead costs for running your business*

Next, price for wholesale before you price for retail, even if you aren't selling to stores. The benefit of selling to wholesale stores is volume orders, even if that means lower profit margin. When you sell direct-to-consumer, you're selling one or two pieces at a time so your markup should be higher. If you don't mark up your products enough, you'll struggle to turn a profit. You always want to price for wholesale first even if you don't think you ever want to sell wholesale. One day, you might change your mind and a great account might order from you. If you don't price correctly right from the beginning, it will be harder to ever sell wholesale or collaborate, harder to raise your prices later, and you'll work more for less. Plus, the biggest rookie mistake newer jewelry designers make is they want to "discount" for wholesale. If you start with the wholesale price first, you'll never be confused about pricing again.

There are five different pricing formulas that we've identified based on the type of jewelry you're making. For instance, a designer selling gold and diamonds would take a different approach than a handmade designer only working in silver with no stones. The perceived value is different as is the price the market will bear. We go in depth into pricing formulas in our Laying the Foundation program. Check out the resources section for more details. To keep it simple, I've included the most basic formula below.

A typical jewelry markup looks like this:

Materials + Labor = Cost of Goods Sold (COGS)

COGS x 2-3 = Wholesale*

Wholesale x 2.5 = Retail

Here's an example for a silver hoop:

Materials: Calculate 6 inches of wire at $1.50/inch = $9

Labor**: 20 minutes to shape and solder at $25/hour = $8.34

COGS = $17.34

Wholesale: $17.34 x 2 = 34.68 (rounded*** up to $36-$40)

Retail: $40 x 2.5 = $100

Here are a few notes of clarification:

*Wholesale markups can run between two and four times the COGS and labor. That markup is determined by perceived value, originality of design, and materials used.

**Labor should be based on the market rate of labor for the type of work you do (or possibly a studio assistant). Do not mark your labor at what you'd like to make per hour, even if you are currently the maker. Many designers find that they like creating first and then decide they want to start a business. However, even if you still consider yourself a Maker, if you want to build a Desired Brand, you have to stop doing it all yourself. That's why I'd encourage you to calculate labor expenses based on the type of work being done. You are the Chief Visionary Officer of your company, not an hourly wage earner.

***If you get an awkward number when you're marking up to wholesale, round up or down as it makes sense. Some work is very labor intensive and the perceived value often isn't there. You can use this information to improve your design process and stream-line the production.

You may have noticed that overhead costs per item are not included in the basic formula presented above. Many makers spend so much time trying to figure out a trivial number to include in each piece instead of understanding the operating costs and break-even point of their business. That information is more powerful because instead of spending time pricing, you can focus on bringing revenue in to hit your break-even and then profit. If you must include overhead in your pieces, check out our Laying the Foundation program's pricing module first. Then avoid the constant deliberation of figuring out your overhead number and estimate it as closely as possible, monitoring and adjusting as you go.

Lastly, if you are selling to wholesale stores and on your own website, do yourself a favor and do not undersell your retailers—underselling is just pricing your product below a regular retail markup over wholesale. Sell your direct-to-consumer pieces at the same prices as a 2.5 times retail markup that most of your stores will follow.

DESIRED BRAND HIGHLIGHT: ALLYSON HAYES

Allyson Hayes of Precious Elements Designs struggled to charge the right price for her jewelry. In fact, her customers and potential customers were savvy shoppers who would often walk into her booth, pick up a piece, and tell her, "You need to charge more." Allyson, however, feared that she would lose sales or repel people if she were to raise her prices.

Then she started being approached by wholesale accounts and her margins were not adequate for selling into stores. That's when she finally thought, *Okay, what do I have to lose?* She went for it and something really incredible happened. Almost immediately, her pieces sold faster because the price matched the level of quality she was providing. Customers had no problem paying $140 for a piece that was previously priced at $65 because they no longer doubted the quality of materials like they had done when her items were priced lower.

That's right, Allyson actually experienced price resistance when the pieces were priced *too* low and that phenomenon has blown her mind. Her business is growing quickly now that she is charging the right price for her jewelry and her customers notice.

In addition to using a pricing formula for your products, you'll need to stay on top of the bigger picture of your finances. We'll go into more depth later in the book when we cover planning, but for now make sure you know your breakeven point, and always strive to increase your profit margins. While these are financial management considerations, they are part of the conversation about pricing and you need to take them into account to make sure you are growing a sustainable and profitable business.

However you tackle your pricing, it's key to do it strategically and in line with your brand. Remember, this is all about creating an aligned Desired Brand. Pricing comes in here not as a task to be checked off, but because it's a way of conveying your brand's perceived value. This is not a one-and-done exercise. Like everything, you will keep revisiting your pricing strategy as your brand evolves.

In fact, you'll keep revisiting the whole of your brand, because as your business grows, so too will your definition of what a Desired Brand looks like. You'll respond to what your Dream Clients are telling you and align with your audience's desires, which is exactly what we're going to cover next.

For more resources on pricing and brand assets, go to DesiredBrandEffect.com/resources.

CHAPTER 4

YOUR AUDIENCE

"Build a lifestyle around your brand and the audience will follow"
— EVA CHEN

We've talked about the elements of a brand and why this is so important in Creating Desire, but how does your brand ensure that you find the right people and get them to buy from you again and again? The key to finding the right audience is understanding who they are, what motivates them to buy, and finding a way to connect with them by communicating what you stand for as a brand and what these people value most.

When you identify and understand your audience, it will help you:

◆ Inform the type of content you use via your marketing channels
◆ Help you stay specific and consistent in your branding and messaging
◆ Accelerate your ability to build a strong, authentic connection to your following.

Target Market vs Dream Client

When you're building a Desired Brand, you have to create a strong connection with your existing customers and those who may be your customers one day—also known as potential customers or prospects. Attracting your prospects and customers starts with understanding exactly who they are and what they want, and refining the details of your messaging and visual branding to make sure you are speaking to them.

Each post on social media, each pair of eyes on your online profiles, every person you meet is a member of your audience. Some of those people are simply members of a general audience or a target market, while others are going to be members of your Dream Audience. Those are the ones we care about the most, and as such, we want to be communicating specifically to them. The biggest problem I see most designers, makers, and artists making when they're trying to attract an audience is that they are worried about losing out on potential customers. So instead of being specific, they end up trying to attract a broad range of customers and speak to everyone. When this happens, your message becomes bland and you end up speaking to no one.

The more specific you get, the easier it is to speak the language of your dream customers, because the ultimate goal is to get the perfect prospect to say, "That's so me!" That's when you know you've found your Dream Client. The magic happens when they can see themselves in your brand, wearing your products, sharing what you do, and becoming a lifelong fan.

Your pieces will never appeal to everyone. However, when you understand the values that are important to your Dream Clients, their sense of style, how they think, what motivates them to buy, and so on, you create polarization and the right people are magnetized to you while the wrong people are repelled.

On the flip side, if you don't fully explore and identify what your Dream Clients have in common, you end up attracting the wrong people to your brand. Clear signs of this include challenging customers who complain about pricing, create problems, and are difficult to please. You'll know when this is happening because you'll feel like you're trying to "sell" to those non-ideal customers instead of being of service. Your marketing will feel more like a push at your prospects instead of a pull into your brand.

You may have also been told to identify a target market but target markets are often way too generic and don't tell you anything about who your Dream Clients are. It's not just about finding just any person to buy your jewelry. It's about finding the right customers, who become the true fans of your brand.

For instance, take the example of a target market of women in their thirties who live in a metropolitan area:

Example 1:

A 31-year-old teacher whose husband is a high school football coach. They have two kids under 12, and live on a fixed household income of $75,000 a year which doesn't go very far in their hometown of Detroit, MI. She has to ask her husband before making purchases of anything "extra" like jewelry to make sure they can fit it into their budget. Most of her jewelry purchases are from Target and Walmart.

Example 2:

A 37-year-old marketing director earning $150,000 a year. She lives in Venice Beach, CA. She's single and a self-purchaser who loves independent fashion designers and buys from the latest and greatest indie designer at trunk shows, boutiques, and local art fairs.

Example 3:

A 39-year-old recent divorcee with three teenagers. She lives in NYC and has enjoyed the comforts of the penthouse her parents left her. She never worked during her marriage and now receives $40,000 a month in alimony and child support checks from her banker ex-husband. Since her divorce, she's decided to pour her time and energy into volunteering for nonprofits dedicated to the arts. She wants to feel desirable and impulsively buys fine jewelry at Bergdorf Goodman to keep up with her socialite friends.

As you can see, each of these examples are women in their thirties who fit that target market, but each of their lives is incredibly different. They have varying levels of disposable income, almost opposing shopping habits and tastes, and they all purchase their jewelry for very different reasons driven by different desires. The description "women in their thirties" gives you a vague idea about the market, but just think about how many women that describes. From the outset, all we know is she's a female and a certain age. Nothing about what makes her get up in the morning, nothing about what keeps her awake at night, nothing about her deepest desires.

The same messaging is not going to resonate with all three of these women, but what should you do instead? Create a detailed avatar or persona of your perfect Dream Client which brings that person to life.

Bringing Your Dream Client to Life

Every brand that creates the Desired Brand Effect has clarity of who their ideal customer is and why they buy from them. That's why a target market is far too broad to create points of distinction and connection with the right people. You want to steer away from generalizations and focus on getting specific, because this Dream Client Avatar informs everything you do from a marketing, sales, and customer service perspective. It also helps you create a deep connection, because you find the intersection of what you stand for as a brand and what these Dream Clients value the most. And to connect deeply, you can't be vague. The way you talk to your grandmother is probably different from how you talk to your best friend. The same goes for different people within a different demographic. Just because you've sold to someone in her seventies and also someone in her twenties doesn't mean that both of these people are your Dream Clients.

Creating an avatar of an imagined Dream Client that is a version of your best customers with a clearly identified persona will allow you to connect on a deeper level. Your brand will evolve around this idealized model of a client and adapt to their wants, needs and desires.

For this to work, your Dream Client needs to be so specific that this person truly comes to life. I'm not just talking about giving them a name, age, and job title, but exploring their personality, identifying their core values, and understanding what drives their behaviors. Once you understand their core values, look for crossovers where their values align with yours. The incredible ripple effect of being specific with these details helps you attract your Dream Clients as well as people who identify with some parts of your avatar but not all.

DESIRED BRAND HIGHLIGHT: ERIN PELICANO JEWELRY

Erin Pelicano at Erin Pelicano Jewelry cultivates a deeply personal connection with her clients. She creates jewelry inspired by life's joys and losses. It's more than just jewelry—it's a memory. Her website reads . . .

"Designing from a personal and thoughtful place in my heart, I start each day with a deep gratitude for my life and my family, and tend to the quiet ache of loss in my heart. I imagine everyone around waking to their own joys and loss—and I strive to inspire these tender pieces of your heart. I create jewelry to celebrate your story; life's collateral beauty."

Erin knows her Dream Clients have pain and joy in their lives, and her jewelry helps them see the beauty in both. Plus, Erin's driving force of designing jewelry for families to treasure has informed her signature mother/daughter sets and generational jewelry for family members of all types.

Your brand will be different from Erin's in the way it goes about this, because the reason your Dream Clients buy from you will be different, but this is one great example of a brand that is truly connected with something very specific in a person's life. Knowing your Dream Client in depth helps cultivate a connection that ends in a truly Desired Brand.

Buying Psychology and Key Motivators

When you focus only on broad identifiers like age and interests, there's too much variety among potential clients, so they never find your brand and say, "Yes, this is for me!" These identifiers are simply demographics—the age, income, gender, race or marital status of potential buyers. In other words, the hard facts. These demographics might help in targeting ads or general marketing because they tell you who the person is from an objective standpoint, but they don't tell you anything about why they buy—about their *desire*.

The real value comes in when you begin to understand a person's hopes, fears, dreams, aspirations, interests, beliefs and desires. They give you the real picture of what this person is like, what they love and hope for in their lives. And if buying jewelry is all about desire, you can see why these aspects are essential in reaching and marketing to your Dream Client.

In order to understand these aspects of your Dream Client, you have to get creative and dive into their life and mind—use your imagination, interview previous ideal customers, model after your friends who emulate your Dream Client, and research real people.

If it helps, you might think of this exercise like writing a dating profile. Have you ever gone on a dating site? Maybe you've noticed that the most attractive profiles are not the ones that simply look good, but the ones who say exactly who they are, who they're looking for and why. You might find a profile that says, "Seeking a high-energy, driven woman who loves to travel and sings karaoke on the weekends." And you might think, "That's so me!" It works in reverse, too. If you are not that person, it's an easy 'no' and nobody wastes their time.

When your Dream Clients visit your website, peruse your collection, read your about page, or see your Instagram posts, you want them to think: *that's so me!* You might believe people buy your products only because they like the design elements, or the quality materials you use, or your proprietary techniques. The truth is it goes a lot deeper than these surface-level elements.

As I've said, people buy from jewelry brands for deeper reasons. As you get into the head of your Dream Client, you begin to anticipate and help fill these needs and desires in their life. Maybe your Dream Client wants to feel beautiful on that first date. Maybe what they wore to a big job interview gave them the confidence to nail it. Maybe the meditation beads and gemstones they bought on their very own Eat-Pray-Love trip are a constant reminder of their power.

Let's look at a few other reasons people might buy jewelry:

- ◆ Sentimental or emotional reasons
- ◆ Celebration of an event or occasion
- ◆ Status or social climbing
- ◆ Personal style, trend, fashion, individuality
- ◆ Healing
- ◆ Meaning or symbolism
- ◆ Attractiveness or enhancement of appearance or beauty
- ◆ Making a statement
- ◆ Gifting
- ◆ Timelessness
- ◆ Values

This list is created to give you ideas, not to limit you! The point is you need to understand why people buy jewelry so that you can identify where your brand fits in the spectrum. Your products might not be the answer to world peace (or maybe they are), but the first step in building a successful business is defining exactly how your pieces will solve your Dream Clients' needs, wants or desires.

Understanding who your Dream Client is and what motivates them to buy builds the platform from which everything else in your brand derives. It will direct you in how to design your collections, how you sell your designs, how you market your brand, and much more.

Perhaps you are already starting to see how powerful your products become when you focus on the intrinsic reasons people buy, but there's one more aspect of why your Dream Clients buy—their fears and purchasing considerations. This list can help you understand your Dream Clients' objections, which is a powerful tool when winning over a customer! If you know why someone might *not* buy from you, you can overcome those fears in your marketing, website copy, customer service responses, and FAQs.

Common fears and considerations that your Dream Clients might have include:

- Price
- Value
- Uniqueness or originality of design
- Trustworthiness, credibility, and confidence in your brand
- Timeliness
- Fair trade, sustainability, or environmental concerns
- Where the products are manufactured or made
- Comfort
- Wearability
- Durability
- Weight
- Return policy

And the list goes on!

When you address these concerns, try to think of them less in general terms and more as fearful thoughts or objections. Think of the objections you've heard from your friends or existing customers. When you make your customer feel heard, you build trust and making sales becomes easy. Here are some examples of what might be running through your Dream Clients' heads:

- What if I don't like it?
- What if it's uncomfortable to wear?
- What if it's cheap and ends up breaking?
- What if I lose it?
- I don't want to get scammed or ripped off. Can I trust them?
- Are their materials really ethically sourced?
- What if everyone else has the same piece? I hate that!
- What if my family heirloom gets messed up during redesign?

Don't be afraid to go deep and get super specific about the internal monologue going on inside the head of your Dream Clients. You almost cannot be too detailed when thinking about what prompts a customer to buy, what holds them back, and what they truly desire deep down. Here's a quick hack to document this as you grow your brand—start to document all of the questions you get when you're out there selling your products at shows, on your website, from retail accounts, etc. You can start to refine your Dream Client avatar.

Designing for Your Dream Client's Life and Style

Another reason I'm having you understand your Dream Client's personality before their fashion sense is a practical one. Some designers get caught up designing a certain style that ends up being totally wrong for their Dream Client's life. Then they realize they either need to change their definition of their Dream Client—and direct their marketing to a completely different audience—or they need to change the style of their jewelry. They see the disconnect and realize why they're not getting sales, but correcting it will take an awful lot of work at this point. The truth is both your style and your audience's tastes will evolve, but when you find that core intersection of who you design for and what you design, you've completely nailed it.

When I talk with designers who are confident about selling yet are seriously stuck with their sales, it's usually because they're not thinking about their Dream Client holistically. Beyond demographics and desires, you need to understand how your Dream Client lives. Their tastes are not arbitrary or unrelated to their day-to-day life. Style impacts a person's life, and their life impacts their style.

One way to marry these together is to find out who they identify with and who they want to become by looking at your Dream Client's influences. This not only a major indicator of their personality, but who they aspire to be, so it's crucial to explore:

◆ Your Dream Client's fashion, celebrity, and style icons
◆ Where and how your Dream Client consumes media
◆ How your Dream Client's hobbies and interests influence their
fashion sense

Once you have an understanding of the personality and influences of your Dream Client, you can decide what their sense of style is based on that. It's not enough to know that your prospects and customers "like diamonds." The woman who wears a pair of subtle diamond studs is very different from the woman who wears huge chandelier diamond earrings. They might both like diamonds and high quality jewelry, but their style is completely opposite.

Example Avatar

I hope by now you are convinced of the value of doing this detailed work and how it will truly pay off when you get it right. To illustrate the depth you can go into, let me share my own example of a Dream Client that I created for my jewelry business.

Meet Kate:

Kate is 45, lives in NYC and is the creative director of an independent mid-level advertising firm. She is super creative but also understands business. She's always had a strong sense of personal style and she expresses her individuality through fashion and jewelry. One of her biggest fears in life is showing up and blending into the crowd or showing up wearing the same thing as one of her best friends. She loves jewelry and is a collector. She believes in quality over quantity and would rather have a few very special pieces than a lot of cheap stuff.

Traveling is her zen place. She loves experiencing new cultures and inspiration from exotic places. She also loves to collect jewelry and gemstones when she travels. She picked up a few pieces in Sri Lanka a few years ago and has been looking for someone who can turn these beauties into a ring and a necklace.

Her grandmother passed away a few years ago, and she was devastated because she had a very special relationship with her. She inherited a few pieces of jewelry from the 1980s from her grandma. The jewelry is hideous and she never wears it as is, although she's thought of taking the stones out and making a new piece ... but she doesn't trust those jewelers on 47th Street.

She has a tight relationship with her family. She has two siblings, a sister and a brother. She doesn't get along great with her sister-in-law, and it's a source of contention that her brother might give her one of grandma's pieces. Her sister-in-law is not technically family, and they only have a boy, so it's not like it can be passed along to their daughter. Her sister and her are on the same page, but such is life.

Her biggest fear is not finding a jeweler who she can trust to get her sense of style. As a deeply spiritual person, she wants to find someone who understands how important these pieces are to her. She wants to meet a jeweler who is a designer at heart and can come up with something unique instead of something basic that everyone else has.

To get even more clarity on who your Dream Client is and how you can serve them, be sure to check out our course Laying the Foundation, where we take you through an in-depth exploration and questionnaire to help you get clear on your avatar and connect that with the reasons that a person would buy from you. If you'd like a little customer clarity, take our mini course, the Dream Client Clarity Kit. You'll find the details in the resources section.

How Many Dream Client Avatars Should You Create?

The biggest temptation for start-up brands is a desire to avoid limiting themselves by identifying just one Dream Client. This can be confusing until you have enough historical sales information, you've been in business for a while, or you have distinctly different product lines that cater to different customer bases. For instance, my first jewelry company had a ready-to-wear demi-fine, personal collection, a fine jewelry collection, and a men's line. As I leaned into the buying habits of these brands, I was able to identify four separate Dream Client avatars—one for my TMD women's collection, one for my fine jewelry collection, and two for my TMD men's line. It might seem odd that I had two for the men's line; however, I had men and women buying that collection, so it made sense.

If you're just starting to hone in on this, start by identifying just *one* Dream Client and lean into that. Remember, your Dream Client is a living, breathing avatar that can be refined, updated, and changed as you learn more about the buying habits of your actual customer base. Once you have that data, you can start developing alternative personas to target.

How Many Dream Clients Do You Need?

Many jewelry artists get overwhelmed because they think they need massive numbers of Dream Clients to have a successful business, but you actually don't need to keep finding a bunch of new customers. If that was necessary, jewelry companies would exhaust their time and resources very quickly. Instead, there is a better way that doesn't require you to keep hunting for customers or finding the next bright shiny marketing strategy to implement. One where you aim to make most of your revenue from a small proportion of your customer base, which makes it a lot easier to build a business and grow your sales with people who already love everything you do and buy from you every season.

1000 True Fans

Author and editor Kevin Kelly calls this phenomenon the 1000 True Fans income model. The idea of collecting 1000 True Fans is that you don't need to keep searching for new customers. You just have to do a good job of attracting those True Fans who will advocate for your products, not only by becoming loyal repeat customers, but also by raving about you and sharing what you do with their friends and followers. You may also hear this being referred to as the 80/20 rule, where 80% of your revenue comes from the top 20% of buyers in your audience.

These numbers are representative, rather than exact, and you will have to do a little simple math to figure out how many True Fans you need for your products, profit margins and price points to make the level of income you desire. The example that Kelly gives in his article is this: if you had 1000 people spending just $100 dollars each every single year, you would make $100,000. I recognize that different jewelry businesses have different goals and price points, so please know that you can change this metric based on your business model, price-point, desired revenue targets, overall marketing strategy, and the number of people you want to serve.

For now, we'll focus on attracting those first 100, 200, or even 1000 True Fans, customers who are not only enthusiastic about your brand, but committed for the long haul. You collect these fans by creating the Desired Brand Effect for your business and taking your True Fans on the journey of your brand. The best part? When you do this right, your True Fans become your brand advocates and share everything you do with their network. The effects are compounding.

Phases of Brand Awareness

Here are the key stages of brand awareness or the steps that a potential customer goes through before they make a decision to buy from you (and eventually become a true fan):

Know — aka the **Awareness Phase**. This is the first encounter a potential customer has with your business. In this stage, your job is to introduce your brand to the prospect and help them understand if what you offer solves the problem they have or fulfills the desire they have.

Like — aka the **Consideration Phase**. After a prospect is aware of what you have to offer, it's your job to create a connection or an affinity with them. There's already buyer awareness and your customer is considering different options at this phase, so the bigger the connection the greater the desire to purchase from you.

Trust — aka the **Decision Phase**. During this phase, a customer is ready to make a purchase—if they trust you—and they go through a decision-making process, resulting in a choice to buy your product

Buy — aka the **Purchase and Post-Purchase Phase**. What happens after a customer purchases from you is just as important as converting a prospect into a customer. Your job is to surprise and delight your new customers here, because then you have a massive opportunity to get repeat sales from this customer.

Loyalty — aka **Creating True Fans and Brand Advocates**. It is well-known that the cost of finding a new customer is 10 times more than selling to an existing customer. That's why your job here is to create an awesome experience for your customers so that they buy from you again and share everything you do with their network.

Also known as the Buyer Journey, these phases are the pillars of all of your marketing and sales activities. That's why it's important that you understand how to connect with what matters most to your Dream Clients at every phase in the journey.

Brand awareness is having people know our brand, like our brand, and begin to trust our brand before they buy. These aspects can be done in almost infinite ways.

People may get to know us through social media, find us through a friend's recommendation, or first encounter us through an ad or an influencer collaboration where we're getting exposure. They might be looking for something and the SEO on our website lands us on the first page of their search. No matter the initial touchpoint where the prospect comes to know about our brand, the important part is to work on creating a connection and speaking in your Dream Client's language.

This next part relates to how you speak to the world about your brand and is directly related to the content you create. This can be really fun, because you start bonding with real people. Maybe you make them laugh. Maybe you get them to resonate with something that happens in your life. Maybe you demonstrate the values that you stand for as a company. As a designer, your story and the brand voice are the things that actually differentiate you from other brands. Your brand voice, messaging, and story allow you to connect with your Dream Clients and get them to like you.

People like your brand because you hold shared values or vision with them. As an independent designer, there is a fine line between your personal values and your brand values, so at times we might interchange them. (We'll cover these foundational pieces of building your brand in the next chapter on brand voice, story, and messaging.) You develop trust with your potential customers with social proof. This comes in the form of press and media coverage, product reviews, customer testimonials, case studies, press, product placements or features, social media mentions, and anywhere you're being spoken about online and off. How you position yourself and your brand is also a form of social proof when you confidently put yourself out there. All of these show that you are a brand that's worth buying from.

How can you build the Buyer Journey into your brand so that a Dream Client buys, stays, and becomes a True Fan? The answer is truly understanding who, what, when, where and why:

- Who is your Dream Client?
- What type of content does your Dream Client want to see from you?
- When is the best time to connect with them?
- Where does your Dream Client spend their time online?
- Why are you targeting them specifically?

In essence, having the deep dive detail about your Dream Clients is important in order to communicate convincingly and clearly to your audience, a pool of potential customers who love and share what you do. When you have an audience that is engaged and raving about you, these fans do the heavy-lifting of your marketing for you. Getting your customers to talk about what you do spontaneously, without you having to do the work or asking them to share is an art that we will go into in greater detail in the next section on Sharing Desire.

CHAPTER 5

YOUR BRAND VOICE

"Always leave them wanting more."
— WALT DISNEY

Here's the brutal truth. There's a lot of competition in the jewelry industry. With the rise of Etsy and other aggregate third-party platforms, just about anyone and their mother can be a jewelry maker or call themselves an artist. While that is great in so many ways, because the barrier to entry is low, the challenge for new makers coming onto the scene is being able to stand out in a heavily saturated market. You want to be different, noticeable, and unforgettable in the eyes of your Dream Clients. You're the creator of some pretty gorgeous things, and you want people to notice them!

Here's another truth. There are potential customers everywhere. You just need to know how to connect with them. To do that, you need to use your brand voice to position yourself as different from all the other design-ers out there, attract the right people, and get the exposure you need to support your sales goals and your vision of success. When all of these aspects align, we call it being "on brand."

In order to dial this in, you'll need to have a clearly defined reason for doing what you do, strong core values, and a mission and vision statement that places your perfect customer at the center of your story. These elements inform everything you do from a communication and messaging standpoint. This includes everything from the personality of your brand, your brand story, and anything where there's written copy like your website, artist bio, about page, email and social media marketing, and overall brand messaging. It's about creating communication and a personality that connects and resonates with your Dream Clients.

When all of these pieces come together, you build the kind of brand awareness with your current and prospective Dream Clients that we talked about in the last chapter. Your customers will feel a connection with your brand that leads them to buy. You know you've created that deep connection because you'll notice it becomes easy to make consistent, predictable sales from the right people. If you're Creating Desire by truly connecting with your potential customers, it becomes inevitable that your customers will want to share your products with their friends and family. Sharing Desire will happen naturally because you have attracted the right kind of customers.

Effortlessly positioning your brand for success starts by defining the who, as referenced in the Dream Client avatar section, the what, and the why of your brand, which together make up your Desired Sharing Proposition.

Desired Sharing Proposition

Unique Selling Proposition or USP is an advertising term used to differentiate products within a niche or field. Your USP is that key differentiator—that special aspect of your work—that sets you apart from others in your industry. A few decades ago, maybe that would have been enough to stand out from the crowd, but today with the market more crowded than ever and innumerable brands that can claim the exact same USP as you, suddenly your USP doesn't look so unique. For example, many makers claim the USP of handmade jewelry made from recycled metals. With so many makers flooding the market, differentiating your brand based on a USP of handmade jewelry alone has become almost impossible—because chances are someone else is saying the exact same thing about their work that you are about yours.

That's why you need a Desired Sharing Proposition or DSP, a more powerful way of positioning yourself in a way that evokes emotion and a connection rather than the traditional USP that places your Dream Client front and center. As a brand, the emotional connection to your work is hugely important. You need your customers to feel emotionally drawn to your brand aesthetics, your story, your values, and you personally. When your brand resonates strongly with them, they will always remember that feeling. By honing your DSP, your brand fills a void in your customers, giving them the feeling they're looking for. When they see their values reflected in yours, what we call Core Crossover Values, they'll get excited to share your brand and talk about it with their friends.

Let's take a look at the components of your DSP, so that you can craft them into something irresistible.

Mission and Vision

If you're trying to create the Desired Brand Effect, it's really important to create a solid company mission and vision statement. While they are somewhat similar, you can think of your mission statement as what you stand for and your vision statement as where you're going as a company. Your company mission includes your standards, the stakes you put in the ground, and your values. Your vision statement is a roadmap of where you see your company going, including your future impact, goals, milestones, and initiatives that transform the company and make a lasting impact in society.

Your vision and mission are built on the core values of your brand. As your business evolves, it's okay for your vision and mission to evolve with it. For instance, you might outgrow your vision because you've achieved it or what once mattered to you has evolved over time.

Example: A company's mission might be: "To build an ethical jewelry business that promotes sustainable practices and lessens the environmental impact of mining in the world." Their vision is: "To be the industry leader in responsibility and sustainable sourcing by working with fair trade artisanal miners."

Core Values

Your core values are your company's guiding principles that influence everything you do as a business. Typically, you'll focus on five to eight core values to build a solid foundation. They guide your decision-making to help you stay aligned and are a good way of checking in any time you're tempted to compromise on what you stand for in order to make money. These core values should crossover with what matters most to your dream audience as well, and that's why identifying Core Crossover Values by taking your company core values to the next level can be powerful both in brand positioning and attracting a Dream Client.

Example: The company's mission and vision center on a few core values that also matter to their dream audience, including sustainability and ethically-made, fair-trade, local, and beautiful design. The brand is aiming to attract 35 year-old millennials who who love sustainable and responsibly-sourced jewelry and products. It might also guide the decision-making process of the company to invest in used machinery, recycle their scrap materials, and donate 10% of their profits to environmental causes.

It all comes together in a way that is appealing to very specific people: their Dream Clients!

A DSP built on values will foster strong connections between you and your customers. It ensures that you, as a brand, can create products that align with your principles. As a result, your customers know they can continue to buy products that align with theirs.

When people read about the vision and mission of your company, your goals, and the future you envision, they'll either buy into that idea or they won't. That's how you magnetize the right people to your brand! Equally, some people will read your company vision and say "no thanks," and that's totally OK because you want to polarize the wrong people to magnetize the right people.

Communicating Why You Do What You Do

Building a business is hard work and is not for the faint of heart. In fact, according to Investopedia, 20% of small businesses fail in the first year, 50% by year five, and 33% don't make it past 10 years. These statistics are not to discourage you, because building your dream is totally worth it. Because the financial reward and the lifestyle freedom will come after you put the hard work and sweat equity in, having a deep, meaningful reason for building your business helps you keep going when things get rough. However, it also helps with something else: communicating 'why' your business exists on a fundamental level and connecting on that emotional level with your audience.

According to speaker and author Simon Sinek, "Great successful brands that inspire, communicate their 'why' first, instead of the how or the what." Learning this changed how I viewed my business forever, because it helped me delve deep into what made my customers connect with my brand.

In his book *Start With Why*, Sinek explained a concept called the

Golden Circle. This looks like three concentric circles with 'why' at the center, 'how' in the middle layer, and 'what' at the outmost layer. While most companies focus their marketing on the 'what,' Sinek suggests that savvy and successful companies concentrate on helping their customers reach the middle of that golden circle and understand their 'why.'

Following this principle, instead of telling my prospective clients:

I'm a private jeweler who is commissioned for my fine jewelry.

I work one-on-one with my clients to create sentimental and beautiful pieces.

Wanna buy one?

By starting with 'why,' I transform my message into something deeper:

I believe that jewelry is an extension of one's soul and a reminder of the people, places, and memories that shape our reality.

My approach to design is intuitive. Personal connection is the key to creativity and that's how I tap into the core of my customers' desires.

Through personal connection and inspiration, I design beautiful pieces that add value to my customers and make them say, "That's so me!"

I just happen to make amazing jewelry!

Even though these mean the same thing, there is more emotional connection when I start with 'why.' I suggest watching Sinek's TED talk and trying this exercise for yourself, so that you can start to figure out how to create an emotional connection. When you focus your marketing solely on your 'what,' it's hard to stay focused on what motivates your Dream Client to buy. When you focus your marketing on your 'why,' it becomes so easy to speak directly to your Dream Client because you're focusing on shared emotions.

Brand Story

Your brand story is arguably one of the most important points of distinction you have as a jewelry maker or designer. It's a necessary and pivotal part of your ability to connect with your Dream Clients, because it's that place where you find the intersection between what you stand for and what matters most to your audience. It creates a bond and a connection! Your brand story is the origin of who you are as a designer. It encompasses your origin story, design inspiration, influences, mission, vision, and core values. Most importantly, it keeps your Dream Clients at the center of that narrative, and how well you do this will impact the success of your brand. As Donald Miller says in his book *Building a Storybrand*, "Your customer is the hero of your story and you are the guide." When creating your brand story, you always want to be putting your customers at the center of your story and consciously thinking to yourself: "What's in it for them?"

Faceless brands are dying. Retail buyers and consumers want to know your story, because stories connect us and differentiate you from other makers. Stories sell. A huge mistake that a lot of designers and brands make when developing a brand story is that they focus solely on themselves instead of using the story as a tool to connect with their audience or put their customer at the center of the brand. So they create a long list of accolades, industry training and certifications that are not as interesting to a customer as they are to your peers. Your MFA and GIA certification might be helpful in selling fine jewelry, but most consumers want to know the artist first. Consumers, especially those who don't consider themselves creative, are fascinated by your process much more than you think. While a long list of accolades might be moderately impressive to build trust, it's not what creates the initial "know-like" connection with your Dream Clients.

Creating your brand story goes way beyond just your credentials. In his book, *Building a Story Brand*, Donald Miller likens your dream customer to a character in a story who has a problem. Your brand is the guide that offers the solution to the problem with a plan that calls them to take action. In other words, your brand story is more about your customer as the hero of your story than it is about you. When you can dial this into your messaging and connect on what matters to the customer encountering your brand, well, that's a recipe for them to say, "That's so me!"

When developing your brand story, you want to start with your dream audience or Dream Client avatar first. Think to yourself: what's in it for them? Your brand story should include:

- ◆ Your origin story
- ◆ Design inspiration
- ◆ Your company mission, vision, and Core Crossover Values
- ◆ Your 'why' for your brand
- ◆ Fun facts that create a connection with your dream audience
- ◆ Your accolades, awards, major media, and training

When these pieces come together, they tell your unique story and experience as a brand, and you create a lasting impression and become the focal point of your Desired Sharing Proposition. Your brand story can be used as a copy on your website, marketing materials, your about page, your artist's bio, marketing channels, to pitch wholesale accounts and the media, and so much more.

If you pour your thought, effort, and heart into the process of crafting your brand story, you can always rely on it to set you apart from the sea of other creative products brands. At the end of the day, Dr. Seuss was right... "There is NO ONE alive that is YOUER than YOU!"

DESIRED BRAND HIGHLIGHT: DEA DIA JEWELRY

Jessica Lawson of Dea Dia Jewelry designs jewelry for outcasts, erm . . . I mean, rebels! She positions her customer as someone who values empowerment, self-love, self-expression, diversity, and inclusivity. She encourages her audience to use her jewelry as a vessel to express their unique nature.

The messaging all over Jessica's website and promotional materials reflects this story. Jessica's story is her own, but it's also about her customers: the rebels and outcasts who took the road less traveled. When you land on her website and her about page, you will either totally vibe with her collection or you won't. A preppy yuppie in Connecticut? Not Jessica's client. A San Francisco hipster? 100 percent!

Once you have this dialed in, your brand story becomes the foundation of your brand voice and the tone in which you communicate to the outside world.

The One Place You Must Tell Your Brand Story

Although your brand story should be communicated through each and every aspect of your website, marketing, social media, and in conversations with your retailers, it's your about page that provides you with a special chance to tell your brand story and show your Dream Client what's in it for them.

Chances are, if a client has found you, they will pretty soon find their way to your about page, as it is one of the most frequently visited pages of any website. Don't miss the opportunity to connect with your Dream Client on this key piece of real estate.

Instead of falling into the trap of turning it into an online resume, take the opportunity to show your heart and passion to your Dream Clients. You might share commonalities or quirky differences that they find interesting. The trick is to give them a taste of what you're all about without sharing every little detail about your life.

Your about page should highlight your brand story while showing how you solve the needs and desires of your Dream Client. It invites them in, allows them to get to know your brand, and gives them the information they need to decide if it's for them or not. Once you've pulled them in, you have the opportunity to share what brought you to where you are today. Give a brief history of you as a designer, and if you can, always link it back to how it might benefit them. Finally, give them an idea of what it's like to work with you, showing them what to expect if they take the next step and buy from you.

DESIRED BRAND HIGHLIGHT:
CIELOMAR JEWELRY

Cielomar Cuevas wrote an excellent example of an about page. She could have easily started this by saying: I design modern, architectural jewelry and stopped there, but she took it a step further to call out her perfect customers. Here's what she wrote instead:

"I design modern architectural jewelry for confident women who own their individuality every day!

WOMEN LIKE YOU WHO...

Have a unique sense of style and love jewelry with a distinctive design aesthetic.

Are tastemakers, lovers of fine craftsmanship and collectors of unique jewelry.

See jewelry as a form of self-expression to highlight your signature style."

She doesn't just show how she fulfils her clients' needs, but she states it boldly, specifying the exact person who is going to resonate with her reasons for creating this product. She makes it easy to opt in or out. Are you a tastemaker too? It's an easy yes or no. Do you express yourself through what you wear? It's super simple to identify if this is a value to you.

Tone

It's not just what you say, but the way you say it that will matter to your customers. Your brand has a voice and a personality.

Whether it's in person or online, each company uses certain words and tone to communicate their message. Think of a brand that is warm and welcoming. Then think of a brand that is dark and mysterious. Now think of a brand that is loud and in your face. What do they all have in common? The tone and voice that each brand uses are so consistent with their DSP that you remember them! You need to create the same memorable impact with your brand.

Here are some questions to start exploring this:

Who is my "dream" audience? And how do they communicate?

What words make me smile?

What words describe my brand and brand personality?

How do those words connect with my branding and assets?

What words do I use when regularly speaking with my customers?

What phrases do I love to use?

What words would I never use?

What phrases make me cringe?

Also consider how you want people to feel when they get your messages. These feelings can be impacted by the way you open or close a greeting, the language you use, the length of your sentences, whether you use slang or prefer proper enunciation, and so much more. Your brand voice includes the quirky phrases you use, how you speak, and how you address the outside world, as well as any special wording that infuses personality into your brand and makes you stand out in a saturated market.

There are so many nuances to communication, but you can keep it simple and develop a signature brand tone and voice by choosing the language your company uses intentionally.

Here are some questions to ask yourself when thinking about what tone you are aiming for:

What questions are you asked all the time?

How do you like to answer them?

How do you bring your copy to life?

Are you more professional or conversational in your communication?

Does your brand evoke humor or is your tone more serious?

When people encounter your brand, how do they describe it?

What are the goals of your website and social media?

How do you use capital letters and punctuation?

How do you express times, dates, and time zones?

Do you use curse words or are they off limits?

You can tell immediately that designers like Jessica Lawson at Dea Dia Jewelry or Cielomar Cuevas at Cielomar Jewelry, for example, have a conversational and kitschy brand voice, whereas Tiffany & Co. is formal and elegant. These elements are important to identify because brands like Cielomar Jewelry and Dea Dia Jewelry are not trying to attract the same customers as Tiffany & Co., and that much is plain as soon as you encounter these brands.

DESIRED BRAND HIGHLIGHT: METAL MARVELS

When lifestyle product and jewelry designer Katie Seller went through a rebrand, she made a conscious decision to be herself and center her brand around her foul mouth. Katie said, "Fuck Off"—literally.

She wanted to break down the ideals of being "lady-like" and just be herself, so she rebranded, and launched her Expletives® Collection. The rest is history. Everything about Metal Marvels revolves around her foul mouth and sense of humor. You see her brand voice splashed all over her website, social media, and products.

I interviewed Katie on the Thrive by Design Podcast in May 2021 and she spoke about this transformation and the impact on her sales. I would definitely recommend listening to the episode by heading over to FlourishThriveAcademy.com/305 for more inspiration. If you're concerned about being yourself and creating a brand voice that is authentically you, think again. It might just be the thing that explodes your sales.

Remember, as an independent designer, your brand is an extension of you. It's more interesting to allow your personality to inform your brand instead of being robotic. *I hereby give you permission to be you.* Once you've settled on your tone and identified your language choices, it is time to look at the visual style, then pull it all together in a brand guide.

Brand Standards

Your brand standards are a set of guidelines for all of the elements of your brand, including your colors, fonts, logos, graphic elements, preferred language or common words, photography, messaging, taglines, communication best practices, FAQs, and the visual branding or style elements we covered in Chapter 3. These guidelines and standards are the glue that holds your brand together.

The reason why this ties into your brand voice is very specific: as you begin to refine your values and what you stand for, consistency in your messaging becomes central to creating trust with your Dream Clients.

Document your brand standards in one place and write down the details of the following:

- Commonly used language, including examples of things written the right way and the wrong way
- An FAQs document with responses to customer service inquiries written in your brand voice
- A one sheet with your fonts, logos, graphic elements, colors, etc.
- A file with all of your logos, vector files, etc.
- A folder of sales and PR content scripts and templates
- Cloud storage for your photos

This speeds up your team's ability to communicate effectively with the outside world, increases productivity, and enhances your Dream Client's experience. It also makes your life easier.

The Cocktail Line

When you have clear messaging, talking about your business is easy. You will always be your best salesperson and brand advocate, so you need to be prepared to share what you do. Have a cocktail line or elevator pitch ready to go at a moment's notice. For these purposes, we'll call this a cocktail line, because I personally prefer to network over a glass of delicious French Rose from Provence over hanging out awkwardly in an elevator. The challenge is to get your cocktail line as succinct as you can! By clearly and concisely communicating what you do and identifying the who, what, and why of your business in a one liner, or 'cocktail line,' it's easy to create interest about your products every day wherever you happen to be.

Using a cocktail line, I sold a custom engagement ring at a dinner party, converted wedding band clients in yoga class, and convinced a stranger over dinner to allow me to reset their grandmother's heirloom sapphire into an everyday ring they love. In the words of Tim Sanders, "Your network is your net worth", so let's get you comfortable talking about what you do.

The cocktail line is the ultimate answer to what you do, why you do it, and who you serve. Practice saying it out loud in front of the mirror, so the next time a shop owner, potential buyer, random person or collector asks what you do, you'll know exactly what to say!

Here are some examples:

"I create statement jewelry for stylish, bold women who love to stand out in a crowd."

"I design jewelry and products with expletives for feminists and female powerhouses."

"I make jewelry with responsibly sourced stones for eco-conscious self-purchasers."

You'll notice I shortened some of my who, what, and why to fit the short format. Remember when we spoke about Core Crossover Values in Chapter 5? Here's one of the places you can use some of them to connect with clients. Play around with developing a cocktail line. In just a few words, dial in exactly what you do, why you do it, and who you serve.

If it doesn't come naturally at first, that's totally normal. It is an art to get your messaging this tight, but you will get used to saying it the more you practice. As you hone your brand voice, messaging, and core values, they will evolve over time just like the evolution of your products, collections, and business as a whole. Throughout this evolution, your messaging and brand story will resonate and connect more and more deeply with your Dream Clients. When you get this right, you stand out in a saturated market and truly create the Desired Brand Effect.

PART TWO:

SHARING
DESIRE

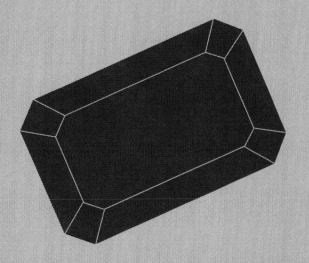

CHAPTER 6

MARKETING

"In marketing I've seen only one strategy that can't miss:
to market to your best customers first."
— JOHN ROMERO

S ales and marketing are the lifeblood of your business, so it's easy to see why this pillar of the methodology is essential to growing a successful Desired Brand. When you become a student of marketing, you market to the right people, get exposure for your brand, the perfect customers flock to you, and you no longer have to stress about where the next sale is coming from. Consistent sales flow in effortlessly.

The goal of this chapter is to give you an overview of how to market your brand in the digital age—these strategies work for online, offline, and multi-stream business models. The key here is to do a few things really well instead of trying to do everything half-assed. By focusing on what comes most naturally and combining that with the strategies that are leading to sales, you'll save a ton of time getting your brand in front of your Dream Clients.

Sales and Marketing — What's the Difference?

Sales and marketing is a huge area to cover in your business primarily because you must always be marketing to make sales. Even though sales and marketing can't live without each other, we've split this section of the Desired Brand Effect model into two chapters. Marketing is the gasoline that fuels the sales engine and keeps your business alive and thriving. Your marketing brings awareness and exposure to your brand, creates an affinity with your audience, and, when done right, builds enough trust to turn people who love what you do into paying customers.

Because they are so interconnected, it might help if we have a couple of definitions to help distinguish between the two. At the very heart of it, sales is the active process of selling your product, and marketing is how you get exposure for your brand so people find out about your products. In both the online and offline world, marketing *drives* sales, so your marketing is the customer-facing engine that leads to any sale.

There are many different ways to market a business. It's important for you to align your business with your values and your why, and clearly communicate "what's in it for your dream customers." No matter which marketing or sales channels you adopt, you must be consistent, create a connection with the audience, and be authentic in your approach. Everything we've defined so far for your brand story, voice, messaging, Dream Client avatar, collection, etc. is used to market your brand.

If you have a business that runs exclusively online, your daily marketing efforts might include: email and text marketing, social media, writing blog content, SEO, advertising, public relations and media placements. If you have a business centered around in-person events and you're participating in trade shows, trunk shows or art fairs, marketing might include: sending out event invitations, event-specific email campaigns, direct mail campaigns, grassroots strategies like booking appointments on the phone or via text to get customers to your booth, or collecting emails at the event to nurture your customers and prospects later. For longer-term exposure, marketing also looks like public relations campaigns, media features, influencer collaborations, celebrity endorsements, and more.

No matter what kind of business you run, marketing channels could be said to be all things digital marketing (email marketing, direct mail, social media, SEO), PR, trade shows, marketing and sales events, paid advertising, media appearances, collaborations, advertising, and old-school grassroots activities. These are all effective ways to get the word out about what you do. The key with any marketing strategy is consistency.

Marketing is everything you do to attract new Dream Clients and get them to know, like, and trust you. Sales is the process of converting someone into a customer and creating so much brand loyalty that those first-time customers become repeat buyers. The next level is continuing to surprise and delight those people so much that they become your True Fans, buying from you every season and becoming brand advocates who share what you do with their friends.

The marketing process is part of the Buyer Journey and it's important to understand *how* you move the customer from a browser to a buyer. You do that by building a relationship and trust with your audience:

- If you're selling online, that relationship might happen on social media or through an email nurture sequence that sells on autopilot when someone opts-in to your email list.
- If you're selling in a brick and mortar retail store, it starts by creating rapport with people walking into your store being curious about what you do and how you can serve them.
- At an event, you show interest every time someone walks into your booth and understand that they don't need help—they might just want to browse your designs.
- If you're selling wholesale, that might look like building awareness about your brand and a relationship, digitally and in person.

In each case, selling is more about being of service than it is going for the jugular. That's why, when you get comfortable and ok with any outcome, it becomes easy to "suggestively" sell authentically.

Owned Marketing

Social media is an amazing tool for marketing and it's revolutionized your ability to reach people who would never encounter your brand otherwise. And you might have noticed, many jewelry entrepreneurs focus the majority of their attention on building and growing a huge following on social media. On the flip side, you don't own the contact information of your social media followers solely by being on a platform. And the danger of a primary focus on social media is that at any given moment, an algorithm could shift or your account could get shut down without notice. I've had students who have lost their entire business because their Facebook, Instagram, and Pinterest accounts were shut down. I've also seen *very* established brands with upwards of 50,000 followers struggle to make sales when these tech giants change their algorithm or favor specific types of content because they've made it nearly impossible for the brand to get in front of their followers.

What these entrepreneurs fail to understand is how to leverage social media to get their prospects and customers to opt in for their email list or owned marketing channels. They end up spending time marketing on someone else's platform, instead of being able to market to them directly, and their sales suffer in the long run.

As an early adopter of Instagram, a jewelry designer I worked with had an insane Instagram following and used that platform to make over 20,000 sales from social media and shows. Most of those people opted into her email list, but she rarely emailed them because she didn't know what to say. All of those customers could have easily purchased from her many times over. I'm not a fan of leaving money on the table so I encouraged her to shift her perspective about email marketing. A solid email marketing strategy and nurture sequence would have increased her average lifetime customer value significantly. When the Instagram algorithm changed, her sales took a dip. Her efforts to reach her customers on Instagram were hindered and her sales suffered. Since she hadn't created an ongoing email marketing strategy, many of her email list subscribers lost interest and stopped opening her emails or opted out of her list.

With so many marketing channels, it can be easy to spend a lot of time, effort, and money on trial and error.

The best way to avoid draining your energy and resources and to algorithm-proof your marketing is to focus on channels that are owned by you, where you have direct contact with your prospects and customers because someone agreed to give you their email address or phone number (often in exchange for something).

The types of marketing channels that I recommend you focus on are:

- Email marketing
- Strategic social media marketing
- SMS text marketing
- SEO and social search
- Grassroots and referral marketing
- Direct mail and call campaigns
- Public relations and media campaigns
- Influencer and brand collaborations
- Paid advertising

Marketing is the process of building the relationship, brand awareness and the know-like-trust factor that leads people into your sales funnel, or process to convert someone into a buyer. As a reminder, the Buyer Journey looks like this:

As you might recall from Chapter 4, the Buyer Journey is defined by the stages of awareness of the consumer of your brand. These are: the Awareness Phase when a consumer first gets to **know** your brand and they're deciding if you solve their problem; Consideration Phase when a consumer is deciding if they actually **like** your brand; the Decision Phase when a consumer is deciding if you're the solution they can **trust**; the Conversion Phase when someone will actually make that commitment and **buy** from you. After this, Phase 5 (and technically Phase 6) are where you build brand **loyalty** and **advocacy**, and investing in creating repeat customers and delivering an amazing customer experience post-purchase is just as important as getting people to buy from you for the first time.

Effective marketers know that they are always marketing through these phases of awareness, moving the buyer along this path. Since marketing is always changing with new technology, and there are so many ways to sell your jewelry and products, the exact mix of marketing strategies you lean into depends on your sales channels.

One thing you *can* count on is that the more impactful your marketing is, the easier sales will be. Whether you sell wholesale, at in-person shows, online, or on your e-commerce website, digital marketing will be the most powerful tool to grow your audience and increase your sales. Plus, when you couple this with more traditional offline marketing like direct mail and call campaigns, you'll see the lasting impact and sales growth. That's why it's extremely important to be strategic with how you use digital marketing so that you're always growing your owned marketing channels (such as your email and SMS marketing list and your list of contacts from stores). Needless to say, in today's climate, it's more important than ever to have a strong online presence and branded website (ideally set up for e-commerce if you have ready-to-wear designs to sell). The more you can link marketing back to your website, the more your dream prospects will find you. Once again, it doesn't matter if you're selling wholesale, direct-to-consumer, in person or on a third-party website. You need a high-converting website so that when people find out about your brand, they can easily find you, contact you, and buy from you.

You might be thinking: *Tracy, where do I start, and how do I figure out what to do next?* The answer is: you need a marketing strategy that backs up your key business objectives. Typically, this strategy can be tied to a sales goal, a new collection launch, a trade show, or another sales event. When your marketing strategy is working, you'll know because you're hitting your sales goals and acquiring new customers on a regular basis. Your website will have a steady flow of traffic that actually converts into sales, and your social media and email list will be growing on a consistent basis. These systems and strategies give your brand stability, because you'll have consistent leads coming in from multiple streams.

It's important that your approach is nuanced and developed specifically for the platform you're marketing on. In his book *Jab, Jab, Jab, Right Hook*, Gary Vaynerchuk explains the purpose of content on different social media platforms. Many brands make the mistake of continually promoting instead of building the know-like-trust factor. They're always right-hooking, so to speak. Instead, smart brands spend more time jabbing by filtering their content through the stages of the Buyer Journey using the KLT factor and creating community around their brand. When it's done right, it becomes easy to get their raving fans ready to buy when they're ready to right hook or ask for the sale.

When you get this right, you'll experience a steady stream of consistent, predictable sales via brand loyalty, aka repeat customers and brand advocates who become your referral partners. That's the brilliance and the reward of dialing in a solid marketing strategy that feeds into your sales funnel.

With that said, let's make a plan.

Your Marketing Plan

Brands that successfully create the Desired Brand Effect in their business know how to market consistently, and that starts with a solid marketing plan. I didn't understand how important it was to have a strategic marketing plan until I realized that throwing spaghetti against the wall wasn't really getting me the result I wanted. Oftentimes when preparing for a trade show or an event, I put more attention on developing the product and getting ready for the show than the strategic marketing it required to get people writing orders at the shows. As trade shows became more of a marketing event, it became apparent that you could no longer just show up and expect to make sales, so there was a big push to use email and direct mail campaigns to set appointments in advance at the shows. In between shows, marketing was primarily focused on public relations and media placements.

When the landscape changed, I learned very quickly from one of my mentors at that time, Marie Forleo, that you always have to be marketing. Digital marketing was the fastest way to build brand awareness and the fastest path to consistency is to have a marketing plan mapped out for all content and marketing channels.

In this section, I want to show you how you can channel your creativity to create that consistency, even if you don't feel that organized around your marketing right now. If you find this a challenge, you can practice it for a while and you will find that creating structure in your marketing plan will help you grow.

Your marketing plan consists of everything that you're doing from a content perspective, an outreach perspective and a marketing perspective. That means mapping out your content strategy, PR strategy, SEO strategy, and advertising efforts on some kind of calendar. You want to plan it out for 30 days and tie it back to your 90-day strategic plan, which is coming up in Chapter 10.

You could create this in a basic spreadsheet, Google Sheets or on Airtable. We have made a sample calendar for you to do this, which you can download at DesiredBrandEffect.com/resources. Best practice would be to host this online in a cloud-based document that your team, if you have one, can access so that any updates happen in real time and you're not hosting different versions on individual computers.

Everything you do to market your business from a content and outreach perspective should go on this calendar. Here are the steps:

1. Identify your primary digital and offline marketing channels.
2. Outline the specific goals you have for each channel.
3. List the tasks or steps and the content pillars that are needed to achieve your goals.
4. Turn the tasks and content pillars into a timeline.
5. Input the timeline in your marketing calendar.

If you're just starting out, the channel to start with is email marketing, because this is a huge part of marketing activity, then work your way into adding all the other channels. Let's take a look at those channels now and identify which ones you will use.

Email Marketing

At any given time, social media sites could shut down or suspend your account and thousands of fans will no longer be in touch with your brand, unless they're on your email list. That's why building an email list is *way* more important than having thousands of followers on any social media site. Your email list gives you a direct line of communication with your customers and prospects, and it guarantees that you can stay in touch with your subscribers, no matter what happens to your social media accounts.

Regardless of what you think about email marketing, it is still one of the most powerful ways to grow an active engaged audience and make sales over time. When you combine it with a social media strategy, you'll build an amazing community of followers. According to OptinMonster, 60% of consumers said that they have purchased something via an email that they received and email marketing is said to yield $44 for each $1 spent, resulting in a 4400% return on investment (ROI). The benefits to your business are undeniable.

The problem is most people don't understand the art of email marketing and send out emails occasionally and randomly, expecting one email to do the heavy lifting for them, instead of nurturing their audience to know, like, and trust them, and converting them into buyers. In this section, I'm going to show you the best ways to build your list and the kinds of emails to send to those email subscribers to get them ready to buy from you.

Strategy Overview

You must always be building your email list. This is extremely important for all the reasons I've mentioned. Not only do you want to grow your list by encouraging people to sign up, but you also want to be developing a relationship with subscribers after they sign up. Nobody wants to sign up for a newsletter just to sign up for a newsletter (so don't call it a newsletter). People get a lot of email, so it's important to be strategic about the offer so that you create excitement about your small business and the products you sell. When someone opts into your email list, they're telling you they're interested in what you create, which means you have to take great care of them in your ongoing emails with them.

There are multiple ways you can do this, but the overall strategy looks like this:

- ◆ Have a system for collecting email addresses and enticing opt-in offers to build your list.
- ◆ Use automation to warm up the leads that opt into your list, capture abandoned carts, create loyalty long after the sale, and remove dead subscribers over time.
- ◆ Use a broadcast email strategy that sells your products while building the know, like, and trust factor for your brand.

These three pieces, when done right, create consistency and sales online and off.

List-Building

Email marketing is a form of owned marketing where you have access to people's contact information. The system for collecting people's email addresses is called an email CRM. Some of the ones we recommend include: Klaviyo, Omnisend, or Mailchimp. Once you've captured their email, you can take them on a journey that develops a connection and affinity with your brand.

You can be as creative in list-building as you are at putting together an appealing and unforgettable reason to opt in. Here are some of the main ones you can use:

Lead magnets AKA opt-in offers: Subscribers sign up for the lead magnet or opt-in offer on your website via the pop-up form. You could try: a free gift or exclusive time-limited sign-up offer, a quiz on a related topic, a product aftercare guide, a VIP insiders club, a promo code for free shipping or a discount code, or a style guide showing how to wear or display your pieces, depending on the product you make. You'll deliver the offer via email.

A compelling opt-in offer or lead magnet piques curiosity and captures interest by delivering some kind of value. Can you see how this is completely different from asking someone to sign up for a boring newsletter? It's not that you won't deliver information in a newsletter fashion at times, sparingly. It does indicate that you are going to give them something of value in return. Your opt-in offer or lead magnet is your way of showing your customers you value them *and* delivers value that they can't get unless they become an insider (AKA subscriber).

A word of caution. Many brands offer a discount code as an opt-in offer. This works well for established brands and when someone is ready to buy. If someone is encountering your brand for the first time and someone is not yet warmed up and ready to buy, you might not get many subscribers. Many emerging brands miss the boat on a lot of potential leads if they only offer a discount for opting in, because they haven't taken time to nurture that know, like, and trust factor. That's why I always recommend my students test several different offers to encourage people to subscribe. In marketing, testing is your BFF; you can do a lot of guessing, but without actual data, you'll likely limit your growth in the long run. So make sure that you're always testing your offers and see what lands with the people who follow you. We go in-depth on how to develop winning opt-in offers in our programs at Flourish & Thrive Academy. Be creative! The sky's the limit with what you can offer as a lead magnet.

Grassroots sign-ups: You encounter people every day who could potentially be subscribers to your email list and help you grow your sales. Go back to basics with a grassroots email list-building effort, which is easy to implement and requires little or no money. In the early days, this may be friends and family and your personal and professional network. Hand out compliment cards that encourage people to visit your website and sign up for your email list (and shop). Do grassroots outreach to previous customers and ask them to share your opt-in offer with their friends and co-workers.

Referral campaign: Create a contest, offer an incentive, or give out a reward for referrals for email list sign-ups (and sales) from your previous customers, friends and family, and others who might be interested in your personal network. There are several tracking software options that are easy to integrate with your email CRM and your website platform (Shopify is the best at this) so that you can track sign-ups and rewards.

Event sign-up sheet: Anytime you are hosting a trunk show, live event, or exhibiting at an art show, it's easy to ask a prospect or customer to sign up for your email list when you're already right there in person having a conversation with them! If you do trade shows, make sure you require a business card or contact information in exchange for a catalog or line sheet. This gives you a reason to follow up after the show manually and via segmented email marketing. Getting sign-ups in person is often a lot easier because they're already getting to know you and love your brand. Write a script for how you're going to ask for their email, then practice it out loud so you don't feel weird or awkward when the time comes.

Content and social media marketing: Content marketing is where you deliver valuable information that gets people engaged with your brand. In the digital marketing age, content marketing includes social media marketing, social search marketing, and blogging. Blogging can be an extremely effective tool for people to find your small business based on SEO keyword searches. For instance, "how to clean silver jewelry with non-toxic chemicals" is a great piece of evergreen content that will not only drive traffic to your website but allow you an opportunity to capture an email address when you have a lead magnet or content upgrade on that page. By offering compelling, free content via your blog, and using SEO keywords relevant to your brand, people will find your website. Once you've led them there, your opt-in (if it's a good one and relevant to the topic covered) will build your email list.

That brings me to social media. There are multiple ways to get people from Instagram or Facebook over to your website to sign up for your email list. You can share the content and lead magnets that you've created in your social media strategy. On Instagram, you can use a link generator like Linktree, Tap Bio, or Campsite to link out to multiple pages, opt-ins, and content on your website. You can also have your web developer create a landing page with a links list that lives on your website (the ultimate goal) instead of using a link generator. On Facebook, you can share your content on your business page, private group, or personal profile to build your email list. You can also host live shopping events that require email list sign-up or VIP status to participate, or provide special incentives for email list subscribers.

Social search: Pinterest is one of the most powerful search tools out there, and because it has a social element with people sharing photos, it's a great way to build your email list and drive traffic to your website. YouTube is already designed with SEO in mind. It's easy to integrate your brand with these platforms and drive traffic to your email list and website.

Think about how you can use social media, social search, previous purchasers, in-person events, friends and family, refer-a-friend, loyalty programs, ads, video marketing, or online groups to get people to sign up. If you're struggling to come up with ideas that work for you, we've made a resource for you with more content marketing ideas. Get the extra resources here: DesiredBrandEffect.com/resources.

Best Practices

Email marketing is the number one way to get qualified leads or warm traffic to your website, because the people on your email list are there because they want to hear from you.

There are a lot of different types of emails you can send out including: broadcast emails, content emails, promotional emails, and automated email sequences that build community around your brand. We're going to break down some of these here.

Each type of email you can send serves a different purpose. However, the main purpose of your email marketing strategy should be to move people along the Desire Journey, helping them know, like, and trust you so that you become their favorite choice.

For most emails, the ultimate goal is to get subscribers to take an action that leads them to your website. The problem is inexperienced marketers end up sending out super long emails that lack focus or direction, and they wonder why their emails aren't doing the heavy lifting for them. Instead, keep your emails *focused* on the task at hand. Having one single focused intention for each email you're sending is important. Brands get this wrong when they send out a hodgepodge of information in an unfocused email that confuses their subscribers. The result is low or no conversion and unsubscribes. If you are sending out regular weekly emails and not getting sales, this is likely the reason.

Effective email marketing balances each of the aspects of know-like-trust. Each email needs a specific objective to do this:

- Are you educating people about your jewelry?
- Are you trying to get someone to attend an event?
- Are you building awareness around your brand?
- Are you trying to sell a product?
- Are you sharing a case study, product review or client story?
- Are you sharing blog content you wrote?
- Are you releasing a new collection or sharing styling advice?

Once you have your specific objective, you'll need to structure your email in a way that gets you the desired outcome. Plus, when you learn how nuanced email marketing can be, you can do a lot of the heavy lifting and selling in the visual aspects of the emails.

Email Types

Not all email marketing is the same, so your email marketing strategy must cover a variety of different types of emails to engage and add value to your subscribers. They all serve a purpose: to build brand awareness and know, like, and trust with your prospects and existing customers. Have fun with this and infuse your brand's personality into the types of emails you deliver.

Automated sequences: This is a series of emails that goes out automatically when someone opts in or takes a specific action. There are three common automated sequences that your jewelry brand must have.

The first is an opt-in or nurture sequence which is a series of three to six automated emails to bring people along the Buyer Journey and nurture your list after they've opted in. The purpose of this sequence is to build know, like and trust and to get first time subscribers to purchase from you. The second is a post-purchase sequence that goes out to buyers after they purchase your products. You create follow-up emails for anyone who buys, thanking them for their purchase, asking for a product review or testimonial, or encouraging them to share a photo of themselves using or wearing the piece they purchased. Over time, you'll continue to nurture them towards another purchase with your newsletters and special offers. The third is an abandoned cart sequence. This is a series of one to three emails designed to recapture people who didn't complete the check-out process. If you have the right formula for these emails, you'll increase your sales on autopilot. Many of our students have reported recapturing 20–35 percent of sales using abandoned cart emails and statistics show that abandoned cart sequences can have as high as a 45% conversion rate.

As your marketing gets more advanced, you can start to build out automated sales funnels based on interests and more specific actions taken by buyers. The idea behind an automated sales funnel is to send someone a series of emails based on a series of actions with the aim of moving them along the Buyer Journey toward a purchase. For instance, you might have automated campaigns that go out specifically to first time buyers a few weeks after their first purchase to incentivize a second order. Or you might have a special sales funnel that only goes out to your top spenders with special incentives or viewing parties.

Once you become a more experienced marketer, it's smart to add additional sequences such as win-back campaigns to re-engage previous buyers or sunset sequences that re-engage or clean off inactive contacts. For instance, let's say you have a buyer who purchased one year ago and they haven't reordered since then. You can tag that person in your email CRM and send them into a sequence of emails that gives them an incentive to purchase for a second time. Another example: perhaps someone hasn't opened your emails for six months to a year. You can send them a series of emails to try to re-engage them or clean them from your email list. You'll need a robust email platform like Klaviyo or Omnisend in order to do this, but there are so many creative things you can do with your sequences once you have that in place.

If you're interested in learning more about how to set these up the right way, check out the resources or go to DesiredBrandEffect. com/resources.

Sales and promotional: These are emails directly selling your products. If you want to make money from email marketing, you have to have regular promotional and sales emails in your strategy. Similar to the jab, jab, jab, right hook philosophy, you can rotate promotional emails with a series of emails that nurture your audience. Effective sales emails have a clear offer that gets subscribers to open and purchase. Keep in mind that consistency is key. In the beginning, if you aren't making sales, you need to keep optimizing and sending out regular promotional emails.

If you're on a budget and can't hire a marketing agency to do this for you, here's a tip that might help you create better promotional emails. Revisit your Dream Client avatar and get clear on this—besides your brand, where are these people shopping? Get on the email list of the bigger brands with larger marketing budgets and watch what they do. How are their emails designed? What makes them appealing to you to shop from? How are they asking their subscribers to take action and inspiring clicks in the emails? What are the subject lines that got you to open? Start noticing what works on you because it likely will work on your Dream Clients, too. Also, if you don't have HTML skills to custom edit your newsletters, graphic design tools like Canva have a ton of templates that you can use to create graphics that can be dropped into a standard email template from your email CRM.

Value-added content: It's important that in your email marketing, you aren't just pitching your subscribers all of the time. With that being said, there is a subtle art of selling without pitching in emails by adding value first. Here's what I mean—focus on rotating your email content through the know-like-trust Buyer Journey. Educate your customers on how to style your jewelry, about your products, and your evolution as a designer—you can even share a behind-the-scenes post of how you designed your new collection. Send out an email sharing your Core Crossover Values and lead subscribers back to your website to read more about your ethos. Make sure that your emails direct people to read the full story on your website via a landing page, a blog, or your e-commerce store.

The goal of our marketing is building awareness about your brand and adding value to your community. If you're only pitching your subscribers to buy, your emails might get ignored. When you can add regular value and educate your subscribers, you give them a reason to open up your emails by creating anticipation and excitement about what you have to say.

Social proof, case studies, and testimonials: Social proof is a powerful way to build trust with your prospects and customers, and what better way to show that you are trustworthy than by sharing case studies, product reviews, testimonials and publicity in your email marketing? Remember, publicity in general is a great way to show you are credible, so make sure you email about any magazine features, dot.com features, TV spots, and influencer and celebrity endorsements. The most powerful social proof comes in the form of happy customers. Sharing case studies (client features or profiles), testimonials (endorsements about your brand), and product reviews are all wonderful ways to show your prospects the experience of your brand when they become a customer. They don't have to take *your* word for it because you have proof from existing fans and clients. .

Event invitations: As you build your email list, you have a captive audience waiting to buy at your next event, whether it's in-person or virtual. You can use your email marketing to invite and capture RSVPs, and remind people of where they can buy, in-person or at a virtual trunk show. Ideally, you want to segment your email list based on location if you're doing in person events because this allows you to target the actual people who might attend.

Loyalty and insider perks: As a product brand, you definitely want to offer loyalty incentive and insider perks, which all can be delivered in your email marketing. You can offer gift cards for birthdays, a first look at new collection launches, behind-the-scenes content, and sneak peek access to sales or new collection drops in advance of everyone else.

These are just a few of the myriad ideas and types of emails you can send. Ideally, you'll be sending a variety and rotating broadcast emails that sell, with value added content and social proof to create "community" around your brand. Remember, the constant hard sell is not the answer here.

Email Structure

All emails can follow a super simple formula and deliver a great result. Keep this in your back pocket the next time you're writing or designing emails for your business. In most cases, the emails for product brands should be focused primarily on visuals instead of lengthy text.

Attention-grabbing subject line: The biggest hurdle is getting your emails opened. Your subject line should pique curiosity and prompt someone to take an action.

Boring: Newsletter 202

Enticing: 3 must-have earrings for the holidays

Hook: The hook is a statement or idea that draws the reader in. It's often teased in the subject line and continued in the beginning of the email using visuals or text.

Example: *The season must-have earrings sold out 12 times* or *The shoulder dusting chandelier earring to make your basic LBD sparkle.*

Beautiful imagery: Product-based email marketing should always be focused on your product. Your images need to be beautiful and ideally you use graphic elements so that they are clickable to shop.

Strong call to action (CTA): The worst mistake many brands make with email marketing is not having a strong, focused call to action. Each email should have only *one primary* CTA. If you want someone to shop from your email, focus on getting them to shop. If you want to get people to an in-person event, focus on getting them to RSVP. If you want to share blog content, a case study or testimonial, focus on driving them to your blog on your website. You can host an additional CTA on your blog that tells them what to do next.

Mistake: Three calls to action in one email, such as "RSVP to my event," "buy my jewelry online," and "read my blog post."

Best practice: Every email has one primary CTA that tells your reader exactly what to do next.

Option to share: Referrals are your best friend. Offer an incentive to get people to share your offer with their friends and family.

Study all of the elements listed above as they relate to your jewelry brand. Some of my personal favorite brands to follow are Carbon 38, Intermix, Journelle, and Lively. These are brands I love to shop, and my customers do, too.

Email Design

Branding is the message you're sending to your subscribers about who you are. Understandably, when you start out, it is tempting to do everything yourself. However, if marketing materials look DIY, your prospects will see your brand as unprofessional. Even early on, I highly recommend using tools like Canva or Photoshop to develop beautiful images to place in your emails. As you grow, you might add a professional graphic designer to your team or find a graphic designer on freelance websites to help you create templates

Create plug-and-play email templates that you can use each time just by swapping out images. Use beautiful stylized photography in your emails and create graphics with strong CTA buttons on them. Visuals work best! Imagine how much more compelling it is to have a graphic with a "Shop the Look" button, rather than linked text.

If you're unsure how to design your emails, get into the head of your Dream Client and sign up to the brands where they like to shop.

Well-known brands with the marketing budget to create this really well are a great source of learning what tactics and strategies work, so you can mirror what they are doing.

Segmentation

You may then want to explore segmenting your email list. Segmentation gives you the opportunity to split your list up into multiple smaller lists, which allow you to segment your list by: location, birthday, actions taken, purchase history, and so much more. It's a great practice to have different lists for wholesale customers and retail customers (you don't want to necessarily send your wholesale accounts a bunch of e-commerce emails). You can send more targeted emails to a specific segment based on your current marketing focus. This feature gives you the chance to send out more emails to targeted audiences and reward your best customers who buy from you regularly with special offers. Plus, it will reduce your unsubscribe rate over time.

Email Frequency

People always ask me how often they should be sending emails and my high level answer is that you should be emailing your list at least once a week, perhaps three times if you are a more advanced marketer. If you want to sell more jewelry online, you should send emails a lot more frequently than you feel like you should!

DESIRED BRAND HIGHLIGHT: KARINA HARRIS OF WAFFLES AND HONEY

When the global pandemic hit, Karina Harris was hit hard with 57 of her in person shows cancelled. As a savvy online marketer, Karina knew that leaning into digital strategies was her ticket to replacing all of her lost trunk show income. So she did something that felt totally off-brand to her: she sent way more emails than she felt comfortable with during her busy Mother's Day season. She coupled this with other online strategies and curbside pick up. During the months of April and May that year, she had a 430% increase in online sales, more than replaced her lost show income, and ended up selling $6000 more that month than her multiple five-figure goal. If you're wondering if sending more strategic emails works, let this be your guide—the answer is yes.

A lot of creative types are worried about bugging their audience by sending too many emails in case they get people unsubscribing from their list. I want you to get over that right now. Think about the last five emails you got from a brand you love. Do you feel like they email you too often? Do you feel obligated to open their emails when you're busy doing other things? We can agree that your Dream Clients will feel the same when they hear from you.

According to Statista, 61% of consumers *like* to hear from brands via email.

The goal is to have people on your list who *want* to be there and who are interested in your brand, so don't take it personally if people are unsubscribing. In the long run, having people unsubscribe when they are no longer interested improves open rates and saves you money on hosting those contacts on your CRM. It's good practice to weed out people who aren't your Dream Client and won't be buying from you anyway.

Of course, if you are seeing a sudden or high number of unsubscribes, this is an indicator that you need to look into the cause, which brings me to tracking. You want to keep looking at what kind of email marketing your subscribers enjoy and what they are responding to or ignoring. Key things to track are open rates, click through rates, and click-to-open rates. When you track that data, analyze the subject lines and the email content that performed well vs. content that underperformed.

Your goal is always to get people back to your website and shopping. Email marketing, when done right, will always be the highest driver of traffic to your website. Get them to your website to opt in, email them, and send them back to your website to buy. That's the basic sequence. The more your list grows, the more specific features you can implement to make the most of your email marketing.

When it comes to online traffic and sales, email marketing is your best friend. There are endless options for using this tool to your advantage. In the beginning, it's all about building your list with a quality opt-in offer and then spending time experimenting to figure out what works best for your brand. Although other marketing tools can help support and grow your business, your email list is the most reliable source of consistent leads. Unlike other marketing avenues, your subscribers will stay with you through the lifespan of your business.

Strategic Social Media Marketing

Over the last decade or so, social media has become so ingrained in our lives and businesses that it's hard not to talk about it when you're building a brand. Social media is an incredible tool, particularly for jewelry businesses. These are visual platforms, making them an ideal environment for creating interest, capturing curiosity, and encouraging sharing for your brand.

Before we go further, I must make an important distinction. Social media is a wonderful place to *connect* with your prospects and customers and build your audience. These spaces give you the opportunity to inspire, converse, and educate! That said, don't fall into the trap of thinking a big social media following is all you need to grow your brand. I have already covered how essential email marketing is, but allow me to reiterate that social media algorithms change quickly and without warning. If you build your entire brand around someone else's platform, you're always at the mercy of their decisions. To mitigate this risk, make sure that you get followers to subscribe to your email and SMS list, so that you can still communicate with them if anything happens to your social media account.

Let's look at how to use social media strategically to expand your audience and grow your sales. It is yet another tool that you need to learn to use effectively to sell directly on the platform using shopping tools and direct message or moving traffic from social media to your website. I've also mentioned that social media is a great way to develop a relationship with your followers.

It's also a great way to move people from social to subscribe to your email list for exclusive content, discounts, and even free stuff. For example, you could post on Instagram about the seasonal trend forecast you just sent to your email list with a link to opt in to download it. You can give your audience a first look at new collections as a perk of being on your email list or host special giveaways once a month for email list subscribers. Share images of happy VIPs who won a giveaway or grabbed that one-of-a-kind that sold in the first five minutes of your new collection launch. People who follow you but aren't on your email list might get FOMO—and they'll be more likely to sign up! Keep this in mind while you work on creating your social media marketing plan.

When building your presence on social media, the last thing you want to do is come off as a promo queen! Make sure you are alternating your content that builds know, like, and trust so that you don't come across as pushy or salesy. You can alternate between funny memes, images of your products, happy customers, PR placements, real-life posts about you and your family, and so on. Be a human, not a robot. Don't think of social media as your own personal billboard. It's a conversation between you and your audience, so make sure you include them in the conversation instead of talking at them.

The most important thing you need to know about social media is to pick a strategy and stick with it. Don't over complicate this or get over-whelmed by all of the options. Whichever platforms you pick, make sure you're familiar with their demographics when you're deciding where to spend your time. With new platforms popping up all the time and appealing to different audiences, part of defining your Dream Client is knowing where they hang out online. To keep this simple, we'll focus on the two leaders in social media, Instagram and Facebook, then discuss Pinterest and YouTube under the topic of social search.

Instagram

Instagram is great for selling any kind of physical product because it's a visual platform. Creating a business profile instead of a personal profile on Instagram gives you access to loads of analytical and shopping tools. Your Instagram posts should be visually engaging and provide your followers with value while still promoting your brand. However, remember that you are using Instagram to move people to your website and build your email list over time. You can also set up Instagram shopping directly on Instagram and links to products via the swipe-up feature in Stories once you have over 10,000 followers. There are also link generator apps where you can link back to multiple places on your website.

Instagram is always changing algorithms and adding new fun features. IG Stories, IGTV and Reels are a great way to get more viewers on your brand than just static posts. You can create story highlights to share more about your brand and feature products, testimonials, press features, etc. Video content is seen by a wider audience than other types of content on Instagram (and most social channels), so play with creating different kinds of videos for all these features.

Ideally, you want to post five to seven times per week on your feed, daily in Stories, and at least once a week on IGTV. Since the algorithm is always changing, please keep educated on the types of content Instagram favors in the feed, for example, there was a leak in 2020 from Instagram stating that Reels content would be favored over static posts in your feed. Remember, algorithms change often so become a student of social media marketing. Each time you post, keep your Dream Client in mind. What would inspire or excite them to read or to watch? How can you bring them some value today?

No matter what you do on Instagram, post regularly and consistently. Each time someone comments on a post or engages with you, respond and engage back! Just like sales, marketing is all about building relationships. Focus less on how many followers you have, and more on how much engagement you have.

DESIRED BRAND HIGHLIGHT: ACID QUEEN JEWELRY

Alex Camacho of Acid Queen Jewelry has a love for creating one-of-a-kind collections. Over the years, she's developed an expert Instagram strategy for selling her exclusive pieces quickly while simultaneously building her email list.

From the moment Alex starts creating a collection, she's generating content for social media, posting behind-the-scenes pictures, videos, and updates. Doing this builds excitement immediately. Just over a week before it's time to launch the collection, she starts releasing glimpses of the finished product and setting expectations with her followers.

Then a date is announced, and it's go-time. Her customers already know that they'll get early access to the new collection if they sign up for her email list. Alex reminds them regularly that if they want a first look at her new one-of-a-kind collection drop, they need to be on her VIP list. Her collections started selling out before they even made it to Instagram, and she's trained her audience to flock to her email list in droves.

She usually sells out of most pieces in 48 hours and sometimes sells out of her collections in 15 minutes with this urgency strategy that she's created. Without missing a beat, she's ready to start planning her next collection for her ever-growing list of true fans.

Facebook

Like Instagram, the idea is to engage your Facebook followers with great content and encourage them to buy. However, Facebook is all about having conversations with people. You can do this on your business page, in groups, or even on your personal profile. Even if you don't use your Facebook business page for sales, you want to have one because without it you won't be able to advertise on Facebook or Instagram when you're ready. You can't run ads from a personal profile. Since video content gets the most reach on Facebook, it's important to use a combination of video and static content to connect with customers and sell, no matter where you are providing that content—on your page, in a group, on your Stories, or on your profile.

If you have the bandwidth and it makes sense for your brand and your audience, hosting a VIP Facebook group can be a great way to build community around your brand. One of our Desired Brand coaches, Chelsea Farmer, is amazing at creating community using a private Facebook group. She has done an incredible job at creating connections, delivering exclusive content, and inspiring her community. Anytime she drops a new product, it sells out very quickly, because she's created a genuine community in her Facebook group.

Virtual Facebook trunk shows are an amazing way to offload extra inventory. You can host them on your business page or in a VIP Facebook group that you create. One of our students, Lisa Lehman, made over $7,000 in two hours, selling through a virtual trunk show hosted on Facebook. Sarah DeAngelo has made virtual events hosted on her business page a huge part of her direct-to-consumer strategy. Both of these designers used their email marketing to get attendance to their virtual events. They really work! (Check out the resources section for two podcast episodes that walk you through the step-by-step).

Your personal page is not off-limits for sharing either. One of our Momentum graduates and fine-jeweler, Christine Stanton Lupo, uses her personal page to capture the moment right before she drops off one of her redesigned heirlooms. She films her customers opening the boxes, and her personal Facebook profile has become a huge source of referrals for her custom jewelry business.

Keep in mind that whenever you're using social media, the goal is to get people back to your website, and ideally, onto your email list. While a business page is awesome for organic content, messenger bots, and live video, you might eventually start running Facebook and Instagram ads and retarget website visitors who didn't buy. You can also target a lookalike audience of your current email subscribers or buyers to find more people like your current customers. More on this in the advertising section.

As you can see, one of the best things about Facebook is its versatility and the number of users, but here's the bottom line with social media. Make sure your audience is on the platform you're thinking of using. Put more bluntly, don't choose a platform where your Dream Client isn't spending time. Research the demographics of the users on the platform and stay up to date with where your customers are hanging out.

SMS Text Marketing

SMS marketing is one of the best ways to get in front of people. Think about your own experience with SMS marketing. How quickly do you open a text when you get one? Most likely as soon as you get it, but almost always within an hour. That's why compelling SMS campaigns are so effective.

During the height of the COVID pandemic, I received several SMS messages a week from a lingerie company called Lively. Their SMS marketing was so good that I purchased no fewer than seven lingerie sets during that period! I was so impressed by the experience because it converts so much higher than email marketing.

Right now, SMS text marketing that uses GIF imagery to create movement and a story with a combination of photos, social proof or reviews, and text can be disruptive, eye-catching, and entertaining. That is key to marketing in this way. When you're crafting your text messages, be clever, have fun, and experiment with it. This is your unique opportunity to capture your brand's voice in a different way by hooking your audience in and getting them to click through to your website.

Remember, mimic what other brands are doing that captures your attention or gets you to buy.

Grassroots Marketing

Grassroots marketing is one of the most overlooked and powerful types of marketing. At first, this can feel a little intimidating or scary because we tend to want to avoid judgement and rejection from the people we know. That fear fails to recognize that we want our friends and acquaintances to be successful, and I'll bet they want the same for you. The people who already know you likely also like and trust you. Assuming that's true, it makes perfect sense that many of them would welcome the opportunity to become your customers and to share what you're doing with their friends and family.

Your friends and family network can be one of the biggest sources of referrals if you know how to make it work. Talking about what you do at events and social gatherings is a great way to flaunt your work and get new customers. I've launched both of my companies by leveraging my network to share my work. By being open about my work, I've landed clients at dinner parties, in yoga class, and even on a plane.

One of my favorite stories of grassroots marketing, which I heard on Cathy Heller's Don't Keep Your Day Job podcast, is John Tabis, the founder of the artisanal flower delivery company Bouqs.com. When he co-founded the company, they had no marketing budget so he went to his network. Using Linked In connections, his personal contact list, and social media friends, he sent out 1,700 emails to his personal and professional network to build his business when he first started. The result of his grassroots strategies was $1.7 million in his first year in business!

I wanted to prove this point to a group of students at a retreat for our Momentum Coaching program. The exercise went like this: I asked them to take out their phone and email or text a client, family member, or acquaintance to follow up on an order, or ask for a sale or referral. We gave them a short script that they could personalize. The results were amazing. Within five minutes, we had collectively made over $16,759, and over the course of the next 48 hours made over $35,235.

You may not have a network of 1,700 people, but even reaching out to 5 people a week or 50 people a month could go a long way in building your network. Reach out to your previous customers, friends, family, colleagues, alumni, and schoolmates. Tell them what you're up to by sending out personalized emails, social direct messages, or text messages. This strategy works, so don't underestimate the power of grassroots marketing!

Direct Mail

When most people think of direct mail, they think of cheesy postcards, old-school marketing tactics, and junk mail that gets tossed in the trash. Yet there's a reason why you keep getting direct mail—it works!! Now, more than ever, consumers enjoy getting personalized mail from brands they love.

One of my favorite brands, Intermix, runs a direct mail campaign for their VIPs. I get gift cards on my birthday and buy-more-save-more promotions for $150 off orders of a certain amount or more. Shortly after I get those offers in the mail, I go shopping!

You don't need to be a huge brand to pull off this type of marketing well. Here are two examples of direct mail strategies that you can borrow and make your own:

Example 1:

Send a thank you note for purchasing from you and include a gift card that can be used by a friend or for themselves. This is a perfect way to create an additional sale and move customers from third-party platforms like Etsy or Amazon Handmade onto your email list and website. It's also a great way to create loyal repeat customers because you're giving them a reason to buy again.

Example 2:

Send a re-engagement direct mail campaign to previous customers from in-person shows and events who haven't been able to make it to shows lately. Include a gift card for a minimum-order purchase on your website for a limited period of time. This provides a reminder and a pathway for previous purchasers to make another purchase today.

The opportunities are endless, so get creative with this one. Pro tip: send an actual card in an envelope so it looks like real mail.

Other Channels

SEO

One of the objectives for selling online is to reach more prospects and customers, which happens when your website is picked up by search engines and traffic flows to your website. That's why search engine optimization (SEO) has become so powerful.

SEO is a useful part of a high-converting website strategy and an important tool for driving organic traffic to your website. While it can sound intimidating, once you learn a few basics, SEO becomes a lot less scary. Having insight into how your Dream Clients find you can be invaluable to sharing your brand with more people just like them.

"Optimizing" in the context of SEO means doing all the stuff that internet search engines have deemed important in order to make your website discoverable. Since about 93% of all internet searches use Google, I'm assuming for the purposes of this section that you'll be tailoring your SEO to make Google happy, rather than any other search engine.

Like all technology, it's always changing, so you will always need to optimize based on new information. However, there are many ways you can actively improve your website so that it ranks high on search engines, even though front page ranking can be tough and competitive.

Here are some SEO steps you can start implementing today:

- ◆ Sign up for Google Search Console and Google Analytics to measure your traffic.
- ◆ Familiarize yourself with keywords, the terms used in your online content in order to improve your ranking on search engines.
- ◆ Choose keywords for your site and research the search volume for those keywords to ensure they are not too broad, meaning there will be lots of competition for ranking high.

- ◆ Get an SEO plugin or tool to hook up to your website.
- ◆ Use your keywords in your product descriptions.
- ◆ Rename all photos on your website to include SEO keywords.
- ◆ Write blog content with titles, headers and body content containing the keywords that your prospects and customers might be searching for. (Don't overdo it, because Google still likes things to be written well.)
- ◆ Monitor your traffic to see what's working. (Warning: This can get quite addictive!)

SEO best practices are constantly evolving, so it's best to do your research. That said, using and understanding long tail keywords is absolutely crucial. In my opinion, whatever your category, trying to get your website to rank on the first page of Google for jewelry will be extremely difficult. It's next to impossible to rank for ultra competitive keywords, like "engagement ring" or "jewelry designer." Long tail keywords are the workaround solution and embracing them will not only save you time and frustration but can ultimately help you make more money from your website.

Notice how I mentioned renaming your product images on your website with keywords people are searching for. If you can get your images to rank on Google Display Network, the images will link back to your website and help drive traffic.

You'll also have a much better time ranking in your local area than if you try to compete with global websites with massive SEO budgets. For instance, one of our students and Desired Brand Coaches, Ana Maria Andricain, has become the number one go-to jewelry designer in her town of Baton Rouge, LA. She's optimized her website for her local area, and has built a huge fanbase of repeat customers in her hometown.

Social Search

Related to SEO, there is a powerful tool for getting traffic to your site and that is social search on platforms like Pinterest and YouTube.

Pinterest is the darling of DIY and shopping. It's become an essential platform for people who are planning weddings, creating special events, designing homes and finding inspiration for just about anything. Ultimately, it's a place where people search for stuff they want to buy—and beautifully crafted stuff in particular.

When you learn Pinterest SEO, you can pin content from your site (and other shoppers can too) to get traffic to your website. Since all pins can be linked, this is an excellent way to drive traffic back to your website. Because of the social sharing aspect of Pinterest, there's a big community and opportunity for your jewelry to get a lot more views and interest. Getting your post featured by an influential pinner can result in massive exposure for your brand. Plus, Pinterest is a great way to build your email list and create content people might be searching for. Remember that lead magnet you created to get email opt-ins? Well, Pinterest is another place to post that for email list-building.

Despite what you might think, YouTube is another great tool for attracting customers(if you're strategic) and getting traffic to your site. Since YouTube is a search engine like Google, video content can often rank higher on a search engine than your website. It's an untapped opportunity for many creatives. You can post video content, testimonial videos, client profiles, how-to videos, style guides, and just about anything you'd post on your own website or other social platforms. The key is using optimized titles, captions, and a strong CTA at the end of each video.

It can seem counterintuitive that a product-based business like jewelry can benefit from having a YouTube channel. However, it's not so much about sharing videos of your jewelry as it is about sharing your brand with your audience. Most people are very visual and prefer to watch a tutorial or video rather than reading a blog post. When people can see you talking about your art, you create a connection. People are more likely to visit your website when they feel connected to you. When you learn how to use keywords and SEO, create community with your channel, and have strong calls to action in your videos, YouTube can become a great way to get traffic to your website and onto your email list!

Publicity and Media

All types of public relations and media placements create massive exposure for your brand. Over time and depending on the type of placement, frequent publicity can generate a lot of sales. Just like everything in business and technology, it's always evolving. Back in the day, a placement in *InStyle* or *Lucky* could drive a ton of sales for the featured products. With the decline of print magazines, publicity looks a little different today.

There are multiple types of publicity including print features, dot com placements, influencer collaborations, celebrity placements, brand partnerships, daily email placements, TV shows and movies, and more.

Publicity should be a part of your robust marketing strategy if you want to attract more targeted customers. Think about what your Dream Clients read or watch, and place yourself there. Then—and this is key—make sure you use social proof snippets to fuel your marketing strategy. PR reps and coaches say that placement is an amazing credibility builder, but what's most important is how you leverage that PR after you get it. You should be sharing your PR engagements—like press mentions and features—all over your website, in your email marketing, on social media, and on social search.

Just like sales, PR is all about building relationships with editors, media professionals, stylists, and producers. It takes time and requires you to be persistent and consistent. In our Laying the Foundation program, we have an entire module where you can go deeper into DIY public relations.

Influencer Collaborations and Celebrity Placements

The rise of social media influencers with massive followings has led to a curiosity about product collaborations or strategic partnerships with influencers and celebrities. While partnerships with influencers and celebrities can be powerful in building social proof, they may not *necessarily* lead to sales.

If you are inclined to partner with an influencer, do you research and focus on micro-influencers with small but dedicated followings. They typically have an audience of people that trust their endorsements. Pro tip: if funds are tight, do not pay to play with an influencer unless you have a known track record with that influencer. The landscape has changed and I'd rather have you focus on partnering with brand ambassadors or affiliates where they earn a commission on sales instead of you paying them to feature their product.

As someone who's had my fair share of celebrity placements, I am so into getting celebrities to wear your designs. However, just like influencer marketing is often pay to play, so are celebrity placements unless you get in with the celebrity's stylist. A celebrity placement will create credibility, and you might get some sales if the celebrity shouts out your brand, but there are no guarantees. Create relationships with stylists and be their go-to when they are dressing up celebs for award season or doing a shoot for Vogue.

Advertising

In the digital age, paid advertising is an important part of a digital marketing strategy (when you have the budget), but not all ads are created equal. Where you advertise depends on a lot of factors, but the most important one is your budget. It can take 90 days or more to see a return on investment from your ads, especially for jewelry brands in a higher price point. Remember, advertising should be used in conjunction with a 360 marketing strategy because smart marketers use ads to build awareness (know), create a connection (like), and share social proof (trust) that turns a cold lead into a customer. That often takes time so it's important to consider options and lean on retargeting website visitors and creating look-alike audiences to your current buyers.

Social media (Facebook, Instagram, Pinterest, TikTok, YouTube) and Google ads are common places to start, as print media and magazines are pretty outdated for creative products brands these days. I'd advise holding off paying for advertising when you're in the early days of your business, but if you'd like to start testing ads, you could start putting aside marketing dollars for later, after you've implemented all of the free options.

When you're ready, the best place to start is with retargeting ads. These are ads that show up on Facebook, Instagram, or Google after someone lands on your website and leaves without purchasing. They're effective when you just start out because they aren't as expensive as cold traffic ads and they often convert faster. Test and play around with other platforms when you've had some success with Facebook and Instagram first.

At least once a month, one of our Momentum, Laying the Foundation, or Diamond Insiders mentees are approached by magazines asking them to participate in a special feature in a magazine for a fee. Don't confuse a paid placement with a press feature. You're essentially buying what's known as an advertorial. These are often disguised as an opportunity to get into high profile magazines like *Vogue* or *InStyle*. Advertorials are paid placements in popular magazines that look something like an editorial placement but because it's an ad, readers can tell the difference and typically ignore them.

You may have noticed that I've primarily focused on digital advertising. The reason is that it has the most longevity and offers the fastest return on ad spend. Traditional advertising in print or trade magazines is a long game so do so sparingly, especially when you're bootstrapping or have a limited marketing budget.

Brand Ambassador and Affiliate Marketing

Brand ambassador programs are a great way to leverage your network, boost your brand's reach, and reward your most loyal customers all in one fell swoop. You may already be familiar with ambassador programs, sometimes called referral programs; they are essentially a system that rewards people who sign up to promote your brand and get other people to make purchases. It's a win-win relationship between you and the ambassador. You get to expand your audience and make more sales, while your ambassadors earn money and rewards for sharing a brand they love with the people in their network. Above all, it fosters a community of loyal fans around your brand, which is invaluable.

An ambassador program offers many of the same benefits as an affiliate program or an influencer collaboration, but there is a distinction. An ambassador program is almost always populated by customers who are deeply loyal to the brand before they become ambassadors, and don't always make a cash commission. An affiliate program is more of a business opportunity, sometimes between two brands, sometimes between a brand and a professional affiliate marketing company. An influencer collaboration is when a brand seeks out someone with a large social media following to promote a product. Sometimes it's a short brand deal, sometimes an ongoing relationship. It's good to be aware of all of these, but for the sake of this section, I'll focus on brand ambassador programs specifically.

There are a few key components of a successful ambassador program. First, how will you incentivize your ambassadors to promote your products and make sales? Here are some typical options:

- ◆ Community recognition
- ◆ Free products
- ◆ VIP access
- ◆ Discounts
- ◆ Store credit

- ◆ Reward points
- ◆ Percentage of sales commission

There's a lot of flexibility here. You can potentially combine incentives and create a tier system where making more sales offers better rewards. If you want to reward your ambassadors financially for making sales, but you're not quite ready to offer a cash commission, offering commissions in the form of store credit can be a nice in-between option.

Of course, it's not just your ambassadors you need to incentivize. What will you give your ambassadors that they can offer to the people they refer to your brand? It's important to come up with an incentive for your ambassadors to offer to customers for two reasons: it makes your ambassadors' job a lot easier, and it gives you a way to track referral sales.

Any kind of offer can work, such as:

- ◆ Free shipping
- ◆ Buy-one-get-one
- ◆ Gift with purchase

Another must-have for an ambassador program is a tracking system—because you have to be able to reward your ambassadors as promised. The most common way to do this, and the one I recommend, is to use custom discount codes or trackable links that are unique to each ambassador. For example, say you have an ambassador named Emily and your customer incentive is a buy-one-get-one 15% off deal. You would simply create a unique gift code like EMILYBOGO15, then be able to track every time a customer makes a purchase with that code.

Lastly, a brand ambassador program will use software for sales tracking, and there are plenty of options that make this super easy to do. Our community members have recommended these Shopify apps that they love: Refersion, GoAffPro, and Referral Candy.

An example of a company that has a really great ambassador program is Pura Vida Jewelry. Not only has their program become extremely popular, but it is an example of best practice as they have all their brand ambassador rules posted publicly to their website, provide a FAQs page specifically for brand ambassadors, and address all possible questions their ambassadors could think to ask. This is a great idea to clear up any miscommunications before they happen. It will also be much easier to recruit ambassadors to your program if they're able to find information on their own.

Another good practice is to outline your goals and desired outcomes before anything else, then design your program around them. Start by making your program as simple as possible, only building out what you need.

Once you have mapped out your program, you'll need to decide who to recruit as ambassadors and how. You have three main networks from which to recruit ambassadors: your grassroots network, your loyal customers and professionals such as influencers, and affiliate marketers.

If you're already fostering a community around your brand, like in a Facebook group, for instance, you may already have people in mind who would make great ambassadors, or you might decide to pitch your ambassador program when a customer buys from you. Perhaps you want to do a formal launch or enrollment period, or you could make it an exclusive invite-only program using other avenues.

Whoever you decide to approach, it's important to be super clear about what you expect from your ambassadors, and what they can expect from you.

Here are some questions to think about:

What are you looking for in brand ambassadors?

How will ambassadors apply to the program?

What perks will they get in return for referrals?

What will they be able to offer potential customers?

What is required of ambassadors?

How will ambassadors get paid or receive their rewards?

Build your requirements into your recruitment drive by asking them for information in the application stage, such as age, location, their online following, their social media activity level, what they have previously bought from you, why they want to be an ambassador, and anything else you think is relevant.

There's no right or wrong way to have potential ambassadors apply to be in your program; it really depends on what's right for your brand. Brand ambassador programs can be highly flexible, and you can get super creative. Keep it simple and clear, spell out the benefits and the basic expectations, and see how this marketing channel can give your brand more exposure and an exciting boost of new eyes on your products.

Trade Shows

Taking your products to wholesale trade shows has a dual purpose and this is one area where marketing and sales crossover. In this day and age, trade shows are often seen as marketing events disguised as a sales event. It's an opportunity for you to meet buyers from boutiques, specialty stores, and department stores around the globe.

If you're interested in expanding your wholesale business and you've never done a tradeshow, here are a few pieces of advice. First, make sure that you research any trade show you're considering before you invest in the show. Are the buyers from the types of stores you want to sell in attending the trade show? Is it a match for the type of jewelry you sell? Second, walk the trade show before you buy in. Get there on the first day to see what the traffic is like and check out the other brands who are exhibiting. Connect with the show coordinator while you're there. Next, build an audience of wholesale accounts before you start doing trade shows. Believe it or not, one of the first questions store buyers ask is: where else do you sell your jewelry? They are asking this question for a few reasons because they want to make sure that you have an established enough business to partner with them and make sure you aren't selling to competing stores and are selling to reputable accounts. Trade shows should be considered a long game in a longer term wholesale strategy and often take a long time to recoup your investment if you don't prepare well.

Once you get into a trade show, you want to make sure you are professional and that you have a beautiful, inviting booth, gorgeous line sheets, a fully developed collection priced for wholesale, and order forms or an ordering application. Spend at least a month before marketing to make appointments during the show with key accounts before the show happens so that you can maximize your impact and sales at the show.

For more trade show best practices, check out the resources section for podcasts and other reference materials from my co-founder and wholesale maven, Robin Kramer.

Fast Content Creation for your Marketing

Marketing your jewelry business is such a huge topic that it's difficult to cover everything in one chapter. Content creation is a huge topic because it covers everything from social media, blogging, email marketing, lead magnet creation, and so much more.

That's why I wanted to give you a simple strategy to develop more content in less time—imagine creating one piece of content and then being able to use it 35 times across different platforms. The Golden Rule with marketing is consistency, and if you feel overwhelmed, chances are you won't be very effective. Consistent marketing is important because it continually keeps your products top of mind to your audience. But the secret is … you don't have to work so hard or spend so much time trying to reinvent the wheel with new ideas for every post and platform. Here's how you can take one core idea and turn it into 35 different pieces of marketing content.

Here's how you do this:

Step #1: Choose a topic for your hero content piece.

Step #2: Shoot a video on that topic.

Step #3: Edit the video and post on Facebook, IGTV, and YouTube.

Step #4: Cut your long form video into short clips for social platforms.

Step #5: Transcribe the long video, turn it into a blog post, and turn that into smaller pieces of content including captions, quotes, etc.

As you start building an arsenal of content, it becomes really easy to continually repurpose old content and mix it in with new content. The process looks like this diagram.

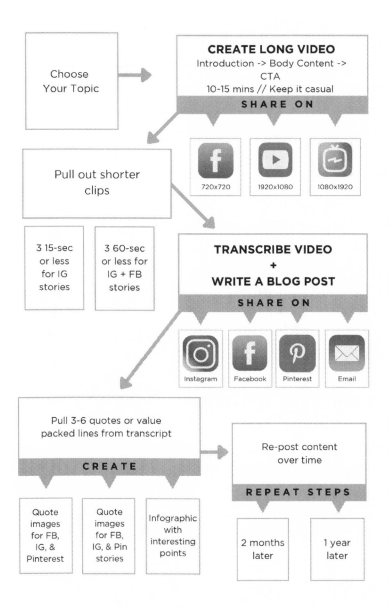

You can download this diagram at DesiredBrandEffect.com/resources. We have an entire module on content creation in our Laying the Foundation program if you'd like to learn how to do this the most efficiently.

Remember to always refer back to the Buyer Journey and filter your content using the Know-Like-Trust-Buy-Loyalty filter.

No matter what stage you are in business—whether you're just starting out, in a growth phase, or at a place to scale your business—you have to *work smarter, not harder.* That's what creating a content batching system will help you do.

Marketing Metrics

What you don't measure can't be improved, and while taking the time to measure marketing metrics is just about the least sexy part of marketing, it's so important for your growth and impact. Have you ever used the phrase, "I tried that and it didn't work for me"? Well, that's why measuring your marketing metrics is essential to understanding what resonates with your audience. There is no one-size-fits-all strategy for anyone. Depending on the behaviors of your Dream Clients, certain marketing tactics might not have the same outcomes for your brand as they do for someone else's business. The only way to know what works for you is to measure the numbers, optimize, and continue to improve conversions.

Important metrics to measure and monitor include:

- Email list growth
- Unsubscribe rates
- Email open rates, click-through rates (CTR), and click to open rates (CTOR)
- Abandoned cart recovery rates
- SMS conversion rates
- Social media followers by platform
- Audience engagement on social media by platform (likes, shares, saves, comments)
- Best posting time by platform

- Website traffic (source and frequency)
- Bounce rates
- Website conversion rates
- Sales by product and type
- Source of the sale
- Return on ad spend
- Conversion rates and return on individual marketing initiatives
- And anything else you believe you should track

If you haven't done so yet, make sure you have Google Analytics hooked up to your website so you can see what's working and what isn't. Use link tracking or UTM codes when you can, and mask the long format URL with a link shortener if you're using UTM codes on public platforms.

Marketing is a huge topic, spanning much more than we can cover in one chapter. A consistent marketing strategy is the fastest way to attract your Dream Client and get repeat sales. We cover marketing in even more depth in our Laying the Foundation and Momentum programs at Flourish & Thrive Academy with topics including email marketing, social media, publicity, SMS text marketing, grassroots strategies, paid ads, content creation, and so much more.

If you're looking for marketing support now for your business, apply for a free strategy audit and determine which Flourish & Thrive program will help you most right now: FlourishThriveAcademy.com/strategy.

CHAPTER 7

SALES

"You don't close a sale, you open a relationship."
— PATRICIA FRIPP

For many creative types, selling your products might induce anxiety or stress or even make you cringe. If this sounds like you, I'm here to give you hope and to tell you that with a little reframe and an authentic approach, you might actually start to enjoy the sales process a bit more. The trick is to think of sales like you're growing a friendship or relationship. Come from a place of service and use it as a tool to educate and entertain. Remember, marketing is the gasoline that fuels the sales engine and is necessary to grow a wildly successful business. While certain parts of the sales and marketing process can be automated or digitized, you're still going to have to talk to people to sell your jewelry, so you might as well lean into becoming your best salesperson instead of resisting it.

No matter what you think about your sales acumen, people love buying from the artist who makes the work. Over the years, I've interviewed and talked to countless store owners and buyers. In almost 90% of cases, the store owners or buyers prefer to work with the artists who make the product as opposed to a salesperson. When I had my wholesale business, the biggest deals, key accounts, and best customers always came from my relationship-building initiatives and not my sales representatives. Even though it didn't feel natural at first, I learned to listen to my customers to guide them along the sales process. So, even if sales is something you'd rather delegate, you will always be the best person for the role. Maybe that's not what you were hoping to hear, but stay with me, because I promise you this can be painless and fun if you're willing to build a little sales confidence.

Let's start building your sales acumen and relationship-building skills.

What if I Don't Like Selling?

Here's the thing—nobody likes to feel rejected! It's my belief that makers, artists, and designers are often so close to their art that even the thought of someone saying *no* makes them feel rejected. Most likely because your creations feel like a part of you. I've been there myself. Remember that time when my then-husband told me I had to make sales or go back to my regular job? Well, I felt like I was going to throw up every time I picked up the phone and called a store or cold-called a potential client. Yes, this was before email or online selling was a thing, so I actually had to pick up the phone and talk to people.

It's important to look at how you're framing sales and understand that a 'no' can mean many things in the eyes of a potential customer. No might mean: it's not the right time, it's lovely but it's not a right fit for my store (or my style) at this time, or it's a no for now (but come back at a later time). Considering all of these reasons for a "no" and the gazillion more that I didn't state, I want to remind you: Someone's decision to buy or not to buy does not define your personal worth as a creator. It's also helpful to realize that the people who say no might not be your Dream Clients. Instead of worrying about being rejected, let's focus on finding the kinds of people and accounts who *love* what you do.

What if you thought about sales as building lasting, authentic relationships with a good friend? What if selling was actually *serving* someone because you're making jewelry they desire and want? What if showing up a bit more in front of your audience is exactly the thing that helped you sell more? When you train yourself to get over your fears of selling and build more sales confidence, you will become your best salesperson and naturally sharing your products with the world will become second nature. Author Daniel Pink describes sales best in his book *To Sell is Human* when he writes, "The purpose of a pitch isn't necessarily to move others immediately to adopt your idea. The purpose is to offer something so compelling that it begins a conversation, brings the other person in as a participant, and eventually arrives at an outcome that appeals to both of you."

That's why I prefer to think of selling as relationship-building, where it grows gradually over time. Think about it in terms of dating, if that helps. You wouldn't say yes to marrying someone on a first date. You'd likely want to get to know the person first and then make a decision if this person was "your person." The same holds true for building a relationship with your customers. The idea is not to ask them for the purchase on your "first date," but to move them along the sales process by being of service, listening to their needs, and fulfilling those needs. With this approach, you might even get excited to have sales conversations with potential clients.

A business coach of mine once told me a story about his father. His dad was a door to door salesman who had figured out that it took nine *nos* to get one *yes*, so every time he got a *no* he celebrated because he knew he was closer to making a sale. I encourage you to adopt this attitude for yourself and you'll see how fun sales can be when it becomes a challenge and a game instead of a dreaded responsibility.

I'm going to state the obvious. Legitimate businesses are profitable and have consistent revenue coming in the door. You can easily create an expensive hobby for yourself if you want to make jewelry for fun and not worry so much about selling your pieces, but the fact that you're reading this book tells me otherwise. The purpose of this chapter is to help you become a better salesperson and eventually train anyone who is selling for your brand the principles you've learned here. Let's shift the way you think about sales and focus on the revenue-generating activities that bring the cash in the door.

If you think I'm immune to this, I'm not. There was a time about six years into my business where I'd had two back-to-back years of flat-lined profits because I was investing in a lot of trade shows and events in the hopes of making more sales. My business was bringing in high six-figure business at the time, and I felt really proud that my jewelry was sold to hundreds of stores around the world. So when my accountant told me: "Tracy, you have an expensive hobby!" Let's just say my ego was more than bruised. Don't think I don't understand your journey—I've been on it.

The lesson I learned from my embarrassing accountant story is that regardless of where you are in your journey, your ultimate goal is to sell more than it costs to run your business. The cool part is that sales can actually be fun if you approach it with curiosity or make it like a game. Shifting your sales mindset might make you feel uncomfortable at first, but it will pay off with practice. I'm here to help you overcome that fear and get into a mindset where you're more focused on what you want, attracting Dream Clients instead of being rejected by the wrong people. So instead of hoping someone will come rescue you, it's time to strengthen your sales confidence muscle and get over any hesitation or fear of putting yourself out there.

Remember, people buy from people (not brands).

The reason this is so great is that there is no one more passionate about what you do than you, so you're in the best position to create those relationships yourself. Instead of spending your energy looking for your perfect salesperson, *you* need to become the perfect salesperson. When you spend the time building strong relationships, you create a compounding effect, the relationships get stronger, and you end up getting first-time customers to buy again and again and again. That's awesome, because it's eight to ten times more expensive to acquire a new customer than it is to sell to a previous customer. That's why profitable businesses focus on cultivating customer relationships over time to get repeat customers for sustained growth. Those relationships are built when you care, listen, and serve to sell. It just requires you to shift your mindset and reframe your fear of rejection, which is the primary reason and excuse that creatives give when justifying why they aren't good salespeople.

Confidence is the most important quality you need to embody to become your best salesperson and the good news is you can learn this!

Here are some indicators of a fear of selling:

Negative self-talk about oneself or the current situation

An avoidance of reaching out, following up, or asking for a sale

Creating ongoing excuses about why goals aren't being met

A lack of focus on revenue generating activities

Labeling introversion as a reason for not being good at sales

Believing in or embracing the starving artist myth

Deep seated beliefs about success, money, and entrepreneurship

If anything on this list resonates with you, here's are a few things that might help you change your situation:

- ◆ Work on your mindset to heal your negative thought patterns
- ◆ Make a commitment to yourself to reach out and follow up with three prospects a day

- ◆ Create an accountability loop so that you are committed to your goals
- ◆ Spend the first part of the day doing revenue generating activities
- ◆ If you're introverted, remember you're creating a relationship and not just selling
- ◆ As Jeff Goins says: Real artists don't starve—they thrive.
- ◆ Heal your deep seated stories and get out of your trauma loop
- ◆ Find a way to gamify the sales process and make it fun

When you come from a place of service, you're solving problems and helping (not selling) your Dream Clients by giving them what they want.

Relationship-building comes down to helping someone you care about. Imagine chatting with your bestie. If she called you up with a dilemma, you'd help her solve it, right? Same goes for your customers. They might need the perfect choker for that special awards dinner they're attending. A boutique owner might need a new product to restock their store during the busy holiday season. A client may need that stunning engagement ring that gets their partner to say yes or a surprise gift for when they're in the doghouse. They might want to feel confident when they ask for a huge promotion or take the leap to start their own business, and that statement necklace you designed is just right. Selling is simply listening to their needs and finding solutions to your customers' problems.

If you need further assurance that it's not personal if someone doesn't buy the first time they hear about or see your collection, know that it takes an average of seven to ten touchpoints for a prospect to become a buyer.

Remember the dating metaphor again here. Let's say you match with someone on Bumble or Hinge, you go on a date, share a bottle of wine, and have a blast. If that person proposed to you on the first night, you'd probably wonder what was wrong with them and go running for the hills. Why? Because they don't know enough about you yet to make that type of decision. No one gets engaged on the first date! That would be weird. When you remember sales is like dating and you realize that a no is not always a no forever, you'll embrace the fact that relationships take time to develop. Many times, a person who is patient in building a relationship will win someone's heart in the long run. The same holds true for you and your customers.

When you take the time to nurture the relationship before and after the first sale, you don't get just one sale—you make a customer for life. A true fan doesn't just buy from you once or even a few times but becomes a walking billboard for your brand when they share your business with all of their friends. As author Jeff Goins says in his book *Real Artists Don't Starve*, "When the right people advocate for your work, your success becomes more likely. Being good is necessary, but it is not sufficient. Skill is a prerequisite for creative success, but talent is only part of the equation. The rest is network."

Translating Your Passion for Your Product Into Sales

As designers, we love to create. One of the most exciting aspects of designing anything is witnessing someone—especially strangers—wearing our pieces. Think about it. Which makes you happier? Making a piece and then tucking it away in a drawer, or hearing someone say "that's so me" and wearing that piece all the time? If you're reading this book, I'm pretty sure you'd prefer to have someone who loves (and wears) what you make.

This is a fantastic opportunity to translate your passion for designing or making your product into sales. It compounds in many ways, because when you are excited about getting your jewelry out there, you connect with Dream Clients who are just as excited about what you make. That's the power of the sharing economy—your customers get compliments on the pieces they wear, they organically talk about the designer when they get those compliments, and they refer people to buy from you. That's what this pillar of the Desired Brand Effect is all about.

Let's imagine you're at brunch with your girlfriends. One of your friends comments that your skin looks amazing! After you relish in the compliment, you spill your secret: you tried out this brand new organic eye cream that has effectively shaved 10 years off your face. They all immediately pull out their phones and order it in between mimosas. And when they get the same result, they share it with their friends. It creates a snowball effect ... or as I call it, the Desired Brand Effect.

When you create desire for your brand, those people who love and share your products do the selling for you. People love to share brands that they love. This is no different for your jewelry. Just think about how this sharing economy builds momentum. If you are building relationships with Dream Clients and surprising and delighting them long after the sale is over, it's only natural that they'll share your brand, which sparks a chain of events that brings in repeat customers and sales.

Before we dive into sales tactics to help you build more confidence, let's talk about some sales channels.

Sales Channels

While you will choose the channel that best aligns with your design approach or business model, there are numerous sales channels through which you can sell your products. The most effective way to build consistent, predictable sales is to get really good at one modality of selling and then add another sales channel once you've mastered the first. Sales channels will overlap and feed into each other, and diversifying your channels will be important so that you aren't overly reliant on one single channel.

Online sales channels are an absolute must, especially in today's world, because the in-person retail landscape was forever changed during the COVID pandemic. Overall, online sales increased 32% in 2020 according to Digital Commerce 360. There is no doubt that you should have a beautifully branded website designed for conversions, regardless of your business model.

Here is a run down of the most common sales channels.

◆ Online — Website
◆ Online — Social Media
◆ Retail store or co-op space
◆ Wholesale
◆ Consignment
◆ In-person events, trunk shows, and art fairs
◆ Third-party platforms (Etsy, Amazon Handmade, etc.)

Leaning into the power of selling online on your own branded website has become more and more important if you want to create a business that survives in any economic climate. Here's why: you can only control your own platform. For instance, you can't control the foot traffic or weather at art shows and in-person events. Wholesale can be very lucrative, but it takes a long time to build. Trade shows are expensive to participate in, and building a big base of wholesale accounts can take a long time. Selling on other platforms like Etsy or Instagram can be great as a second source of revenue, but if it's your primary sales channel, you're putting sales success in the hands of someone else's hands. Your posts might not get pushed out in the algorithm. And the worst of all, you could get shut down for any reason at all and oftentimes you might not even get a reason. You don't own the data on these third-party platforms, so build an anti-fragile business by leaning into a multi-stream business with your emphasis on selling on your own website.

If you don't think this could happen to you, one of my previous mentees came to me to try to help her diversify her revenue streams. She was bringing in about $500,000 a year with the majority of her sales coming from

Etsy. The owners knew the risk of putting their eggs in one basket but got so caught up in the "busy-ness" of their business that they ended up losing it overnight. During Hurricane Maria, their Houston based studio flooded and the power and internet was out for several weeks. Once they got back online, they had an influx of customers who reported the brand to Etsy for not shipping on time. In the midst of a natural disaster, they had no recourse. The husband and wife team had to scramble to find jobs after being entrepreneurs for years, because they didn't move quickly enough.

I'll emphasize again how important it is to have your own direct-to-consumer channel in the mix. Most successful brands have a multi-stream business, meaning they have a branded website, a retail store, participate in live events, and sell wholesale or on other online channels. Setting up your business in this way makes it life-proof and recession-proof, because your business can't suddenly go away overnight when you've spent time growing multiple channels for your customers to buy. Today, you absolutely *must* have a website that becomes your number one sales tool if you want to keep sales flowing in uncertain times.

DESIRED BRAND HIGHLIGHT: EC DESIGN STUDIO

Emily Johnson of EC Design Studio had a successful business selling custom commissions and one-of-a-kind jewelry in person in her studio before she came to us. She was committed to growing her online presence and reaching more clients for her point-and-click website sales. Since she was doing most of the marketing alone, her online sales strategy was often an afterthought or fell by the wayside. I'm sure many solo business owners reading this can relate.

After implementing the digital marketing strategies we taught her via the Desired Brand Effect, Emily started gaining traction online. By getting more strategic and planning out her online marketing in advance, her online sales grew by 2900% in just a year by emailing regularly, being consistent with social media, and by training those in-person studio customers to buy from her online.

The important thing to note here is that offline sales feed into online sales now more than ever. The more you build your online presence, the more your customers will buy. The best part about her growth is that Emily was able to hire another employee to help with her marketing and run her studio so she could focus on the parts of the business that she loved most.

Online — Branded Website

Regardless of whether your primary sales channel is wholesale, a third-party site, or even in-person events, if you don't have a website that's working *for* you, you're leaving money on the table. I recommend that most types of businesses reading this book use their website as one of their primary sales channels.

You can think of your website like a digital postcard or business card that's used for a variety of purposes. In this age of social media and social search engines, your website is a place for traffic to land, for the media to discover if you're a legit brand, for wholesale accounts to stalk you before they decide to buy from you, and for the general public to shop directly from your e-commerce store. You can use it as a place to encourage third-party shoppers to purchase from you again (instead of going back to Etsy) or for wholesale customers to place reorders. You can even include a custom commission or contact form so you can meet prospects from all over the world for your luxury bespoke pieces. It doesn't matter how you sell your products, your website will serve as a tool to speed up authentic, connected conversions with your perfect customers.

DESIRED BRAND HIGHLIGHT: KAJAL NAINA

Many fine jewelers are hesitant about selling online and that's why many of them lean into traditional selling methods like trunk shows, retail stores, and wholesale. Those sales channels can be extremely powerful in growing a business especially when you partner that growth with online sales channels.

Enter: award-winning fine jeweler Kajal Naina. She's a designer who was extremely skeptical about selling fine jewelry online. She had built a successful business selling to retail stores and via in-person trunk shows and figured that most people want to touch and feel the designs first. Even with this hesitation, she was willing to give online a try and developed a campaign to grow her email list audience with a giveaway, land PR opportunities for more exposure and credibility, and create urgency so that when a new collection was launched, people had a reason to buy—online.

Within a few short months of truly going all in with digital marketing, Kajal's online sales skyrocketed and became a solid revenue stream of her own. She shared the results of a new collection drop: "I sold 54 pieces and made $53,000 in 10 days. Today was my second $10,000 day and it feels surreal." So if you're someone who thinks it's challenging to sell fine jewelry online to support your other channels, think again. It works.

Online — Social Media and Social Search

A few short years ago, selling on social media wasn't even a thing. Now, with shoppable apps for Pinterest, Instagram, and Facebook, using social media to sell your jewelry is a great way to leverage sales online. In addition, you can use these tools to sell directly inside the application and to consistently drive traffic to your website.

You can also use social media platforms to host virtual trunk shows. Virtual trunk shows on Facebook have become a Flourish & Thrive Community favorite, often generating $2,000–$39,000 in revenue in as little as two hours. Facebook event pages and Facebook groups make it super easy to host a virtual trunk show. Plus, you can use streaming platforms like Streamyard or selling tools like CommentSold to boost engagement and sales inside your virtual trunk show or social selling event.

Since social media is changing almost every day and giving you the how-to is beyond the scope of this book, I'd love to invite you to subscribe to the Thrive by Design Podcast wherever you listen to podcasts. Every week, I release new episodes on a wide variety of topics. Check out the interviews with successful Flourish & Thrive Academy designers like Lisa

Lehman, Sarah DeAngelo, Shehana Kimiangatau, and Jeana and Jared Rushton about their virtual trunk show and social media tactics. You can access these episodes and more at FlourishThriveAcademy.com/podcast or head over to DesiredBrandEffect.com/resources for more information on virtual trunk shows that sell.

Retail Store or Co-operative Studio Space

Owning a retail store or participating in a shared co-operative studio space is a great way to sell your jewelry along with other brands. You can use your retail store to build a local customer base for your jewelry while introducing other products into the mix for additional revenue. You can also use this as a way to build your email list and website so that you can capture visitors after they leave the local area or send your social media followers to shop the brands you carry (and your jewelry too). One of our graduates, Mallory Shelter of Mallory Shelter Jewelry, started a retail store called Shelter Shop where she sells her own jewelry alongside brands like Melissa Joy Manning, Page Sargisson, and many others.

Another approach is to connect with local artisans and create a retail experience together. You reduce the financial obligation of opening your own store and you create an opportunity for sales collaborations and growth. I love shouting out makers who have graduated from our programs and have built wildly successful brands. One of those makers, Colleen Mauer of Colleen Mauer Designs, participated in a co-operative space in San Francisco alongside other jewelry brands. The designers in the co-op split the responsibility of attending the shop and sold each other's jewelry in the true spirit of #CommunityOverCompetition.

Wholesale

Selling to other retail stores (aka wholesale) is an amazing way to connect with customers who might never find you otherwise. If you're lucky enough to sell to reputable stores, you'll build massive credibility around your brand, increasing your chances of getting media coverage, connecting with stylists, and so much more. Many emerging designers get discouraged quickly when selling to stores because there's a lot of competition for limited shelf space. If you want to do wholesale really well, you need to be positioning your brand as a Desired Brand.

Here are a few tips to maximize your impact selling to stores:

◆ Create a signature style that is unique to you. Derivative design is basic and doesn't position you as a brand that has something new to offer. So make sure you lean into your signature style so you stand out amongst your competition.

◆ Educate yourself on how to price your jewelry right for wholesale before you try to get orders from stores. Most newbies or rookies to wholesale feel offended when retail partners ask for wholesale pricing—they are not asking for a discount, they are asking for wholesale pricing so that they have enough profit margin to run their business. That's why you need to understand how to make a profit while pricing for wholesale before you sell to stores. We have extensive training on wholesale vs. retail pricing in our Laying the Foundation Program.

◆ Make it easy for the stores to sell your work. Create in person or video training and marketing materials to train their salespeople, share your story so that they can educate their customers about it, and act as if you're partnering with your wholesale accounts. If they're successful in selling your work, they'll enjoy working with you and will reorder.

◆ Do your research. Before you start your outreach campaign, make sure that you create a wholesale dream store 'hit' list. Research the store owner, buyer, and the products that the stores carry. Make sure that the look you design in or the product categories you design aren't already covered. Make sure your jewelry sells in the price point range (at retail) comparatively to other jewelry or products that the store carries. For instance, you might find an awesome store that you want to sell to, but they only sell delicate fine jewelry and you design chunky silver rings.

◆ Be patient, persistent and respectful. Of all the sales channels, wholesale relationships take the longest to develop. Keep in mind, in demand stores get hundreds of wholesale inquiries a day. It used to be that you could participate in a trade show and land a bunch of wholesale accounts, make your show fees back, and call it a day. That's not the case anymore, so patience is key. Start in your local area and expand from there.

◆ Be selective and build relationships with the right stores for your brand to keep moving forward.

If you're looking for more wholesale advice, my dear friend and cofounder at Flourish & Thrive Academy, Robin Kramer, is a wholesale expert and loves to mentor students about their wholesale business. Check out the DesiredBrandEffect.com/resources for more information on wholesale.

Consignment

Consignment is my least favorite sales channel because it's similar to wholesale but without the financial commitment to buy your jewelry from the wholesale stores. Many retail stores are moving towards a consignment, on memo, or sale or return model as a way to reduce overhead costs and put the expense on the designer. Less reputable consignment sellers aren't invested in selling your designs if they haven't paid for it upfront, which leads to a "let's see if it sells" attitude instead of a "let's sell these pieces" attitude.

With that being said, selling consignment can work really well when you partner with great stores. You'll need a proper consignment agreement with solid payment terms, schedule for payments (at least once a month), and a commitment to sell to stores with a solid reputation. It might require more frequent check-ins from you, as well. Pro tip: if you have a great relationship with a consignment store, after you've successfully sold through several orders (and get paid), approach them about moving to a wholesale arrangement so that you aren't financing their store's inventory.

In-Person Events

Art shows, craft fairs, trunk shows, home parties, and retail pop-ups are a fantastic way to test products, grow your audience, and build a fan base of Dream Clients in your local area. Highly attended in-person events can be a great source of sales, help build your email list, and increase your overall direct-to-consumer sales if you know how to leverage offline to online sales. Be strategic with the time you spend in front of people at shows to grow your online audience and give them an incentive to shop on your website after the event is done.

Over time, live events might feel exhausting—especially if you're doing them frequently. Setting up and tearing down a booth is a lot of work. Even worse is when you have a bad show because of sideways rain or blistering heat, or a lack of foot traffic or attendance. It can be frustrating and stressful, especially if you were relying on that income to fund your business. This is exactly why you must be strategic about which shows you participate in and use them to grow your online sales after the show.

DESIRED BRAND HIGHLIGHT: JEWEL OF HAVANA

Ana Maria Andricain from Jewel of Havana began her full-time jewelry business after leaving a successful 25-year career as a Broadway actress. She started making jewelry on the side as a creative outlet, but it wasn't long before her fellow performers saw her work and started buying her pieces. When she and her husband moved from NYC to Louisiana, she turned her side hustle into a full-time business.

Ana Maria spent every weekend hitting trade shows, markets, and trunk shows with her beautiful jewelry in tow. She traveled constantly, and it became her primary source of revenue. Even though she was building an email list via her live shows, she wasn't truly leveraging it for online sales. Her business success was completely dependent on her showing up every weekend to live shows. It was exhausting.

Just when everything was going right, she was diagnosed with breast cancer. Bedridden and undergoing treatments, Ana had to cancel most of her shows. She wondered how she was going to keep her business afloat and thriving.

That's when she discovered Flourish & Thrive Academy. Ana Maria took our eight-week Laying the Foundation program and learned how to use live events and shows to grow her email list, nurture her customers (on autopilot), and convert them into online customers. The entire time she was taking care of herself, going through treatments, and kicking cancer's butt!

She also learned how to further develop her collections and price her work correctly, giving her the revenue and profit margin she needed to be more selective with the shows she participated in. She's used live events with online sales modalities to build a thriving 6+ figure business that offers her a lot of flexibility to take January off every year to travel with her husband. Ana Maria has been coaching for Flourish & Thrive Programs for many years now and teaches her offline to online show secrets in our Momentum program.

Third-Party Sites

Third-party websites like Etsy and Amazon Handmade can be awesome sales channels and completely make sense if you're getting a lot of sales from them. The problem is that you put your business at risk if you're only selling on a third-party platform or get most of your sales from it. They are great as a secondary source *and* if you're strategic about getting those customers to opt in to your email list or buy from your branded website the next time they shop from you. The other downside is when someone buys something on Etsy or Amazon, what do they say when someone asks where they bought it? "I bought it on Etsy (or Amazon)!" Which means there is little to no brand loyalty and getting repeat sales is more challenging on these platforms.

These platforms are strict because they want to keep their customers on the platform, where they own the customer info. Technically these customers are not your customers, even though you get paid for the products.

For Etsy customers, include a box insert or ride-along offer to get a free gift on your website (like downloading a product care guide or getting a free polishing cloth) in exchange for their email address. When you do this right, you can start to build your direct sales line with those Dream Clients and avoid the wasted opportunity of your customers saying: "I bought it on Etsy!"

A note of caution: Even if the majority of your sales are coming from a third party platform, beware of placing the success of your business in someone else's hands. As I shared earlier, I've heard horror stories from many designers in our community who have lost their multi six-figure businesses overnight because Amazon or Etsy decided that a designer or brand didn't follow their terms of service. You'll be much better off when you have full control over your sales success through the platforms you control and use third-party platforms as another source of revenue..

Which Sales Channels Are Right for You Now?

Would your business survive if one of your revenue streams went away? This is an important question to ask yourself. You might feel like hiding from your numbers, but evaluating revenue streams is the fastest way to understand how to set goals and to gain clarity on where to focus your time and attention. In Chapter 10, we'll be going deeper into goal-setting and strategic planning for your business. Understanding your current sales channels is the key to making big shifts. When you embrace the numbers, you have the power to make smart decisions. Take a moment right now and look at last year's sales to set yourself up for better sales projections and goal setting.

Step 1: Evaluate current revenue streams

Tracking your sales and revenue streams by sales channel will set you free. If you aren't already doing this, start now. Track sales and identify your top two or three revenue streams. If you can get very specific and even micro-target where your sales are coming from, you can streamline your sales efforts.

Step 2: Evaluate excitement factor

Once you've evaluated your top revenue streams, rate your excitement level for each one on a scale of 1–10. Let's say you hate doing shows, but your best show is bringing in pretty good sales. It might be time to re-evaluate if that's a long-term game plan to keep in the sales mix.

Step 3: Double down on what's working

If you're excited about it and it's working, here is where it gets fun! Put most of your energy into building these revenue streams

As you're deciding on which channels to double down on or ditch, remember that every business needs diversified revenue streams, the most highly leveraged of which is direct-to-consumer sales on your branded website. Yes, selling e-commerce or using your website to attract leads does take strategy, consistent work, and practice. It's not an overnight fix. However, if you stick with it and use your website and online marketing to communicate and sell to your customers, you can life-proof and recession-proof your business so that you have a solid stream of sales coming in.

Once you know where you'll be selling, you can start to create a strategic journey for the buyer to go on. This is what's known as a sales funnel. In its broadest definition, it refers to how you take your potential customer from the stage of being unaware about your brand or products all the way to the point where they can't wait to make a purchase. Remember the graphic I shared earlier—these are stages of the Buyer Journey, or a sales funnel.

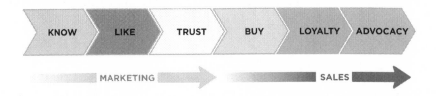

For brands selling in person, that sales funnel might just be a conversation. For brands selling wholesale, that might be a series of phone calls, emails, meetings, etc, to move people along the sales funnel. For brands selling online, it's more narrowly defined as the automated sequences that you consciously build out to help your prospects turn into customers through that journey. We will talk about automation and systems more in depth in Chapter 11. The more you can automate the sales process, the less stressful selling will be, especially if your tech is doing some of the heavy lifting of relationship-building and sales conversations. Of course, another way to build that sales confidence is to reframe your beliefs around selling, which is what we're going to do now.

Come From a Place of Service

Now that you're clear on how you're selling your product, let's talk about how to build sales confidence with sales strategies. If selling is scary to you, it can be helpful to remember what Daniel Pink says: "To sell is human." Let's see if we can get you to that place where you are comfortable persuading and guiding people along the path to a sale without feeling like you're being pushy.

Over time, as you learn to sell with more confidence and understand the key components of the Desire Journey, selling will feel really natural to you, because you are just helping someone out. Great sales people are problem solvers. When you start understanding how you can solve problems with your products, creating an authentic connection, aligning on core-crossover values, and building trust happens by just helping your prospects and customers out. There's a lot to unpack here and many shades of nuance, which is why I want to remind you that throughout the sales process, your job is to educate, entertain, and inform.

One of the reasons we talk about sales in the framework of the sharing economy is that when you're doing this right, you're creating a connection that turns people into first-time customers and eventually into repeat customers. When you come from a place of service with your sales efforts, your customers won't even realize you're selling (and neither will you) because you're helping to deliver something they need and want.

Remember, great salespeople are problem-solvers, so when you start to think about selling as solving people's problems, it takes the anxiety, stress, and fear out of it. Let's highlight a few scenarios that can help you see how selling can solve problems.

Scenario 1:

Problem: You're trying to reach more customers on Instagram. You're getting a bunch of "I love it!" comments on the post and tons of likes, but for some reason you aren't making sales on the platform.

Issue: You can't figure out why people aren't buying, especially because you get likes and comments on your posts.

Reframe: People love to scroll social media as a distraction, so think of your social media posts as an introduction to your designs. If you aren't getting the results you want, perhaps there's a different way to engage your social audience to talk 'with' them instead of talking 'at' them.

Service solution: Remember, social media sales can come fast but more often than not, it takes a bit more time. Create captions that engage your audience by asking easy to answer questions. Reply to every comment on your posts. If your conversation in the comments is going somewhere, bring it to direct messages. Even if you don't make a sale right away, your followers will notice that you care about them.

Scenario 2:

Problem: Your best wholesale account hasn't reordered in three months. You know they've sold out of your product and they aren't responding to your emails. Every time you call, they say they'll call tomorrow, but you never hear from them.

Issue: You feel ignored and confused. You're afraid the buyer doesn't want to reorder because she doesn't like working with you.

Reframe: More often than not, a buyer's lack of response has nothing to do with you or your product. They're busy, they forgot to reorder, and they have a million other things going on.

Service Solution: Solve their problem! Make it easy for them by writing up a sample reorder. Tell them they just need to reply with a "yes" or "no" and you'll get the order filled.

Scenario 3:

Problem: You know your customer needs a gift for his wife in three days, and you only do made-to-order one-of-a-kind jewelry. You've told him it takes two weeks to get most products completed. He can't make a decision and is slow to respond.

Issue: You're afraid he doesn't actually want to work with you again. You don't want to be pushy or annoy him because he's been a good customer.

Reframe: He's just really busy at work, but does want to surprise his wife. It's stressful because she always tells him he's not a good gift-giver. So he puts it off because he doesn't want to make the wrong decision.

Service Solution: You email him and offer to create a custom-design gift package experience where his wife can work with you to create the piece of her dreams. Also, you write down her birthday and send him a note 6–8 weeks in advance next year.

Scenario 4:

Problem: You get a message from a customer on your website who loves your jewelry but they aren't sure what to order because they can't tell the size and scale of the pieces. You emailed them back, but you haven't heard from them. Your abandoned cart sequence isn't even converting the customer.

Issue: You feel like this online sales thing isn't working for you, even though you would prefer to sell on your website because you're an introvert.

Reframe: More often than not, people are getting a lot of emails and may not have seen yours come in.

Service Solution: Send them an email from your personal email account (not from your CRM) and offer to do a video call where you model the samples so she can see the size and scale. This is a great opportunity to show how the bags can work together with other products that she might be interested in.

When you come from a place of service, selling is not a dirty word! You're solving their problems, no matter how big or small. It's all about putting yourself in the shoes of your Dream Clients, understanding how to solve their problems, and making it easy for them to buy your products! The best way to understand their problems is simply by listening.

Tactical Sales Skills

Becoming your best salesperson, even as an introvert, is a lot easier than you think. As we mentioned in the previous section, it starts by understanding how you can solve a problem. More so, it's about being in control of the conversation and guiding the person to make a purchase. It's not rocket science, but it does take practice so I want to guide you through some ways to sell without selling in a sales conversation.

Develop rapport

Find a way to connect with your customer before you try to sell them. Having a way to connect on something that matters to them is important. If you know something about the person in advance, connect with them. Robin Kramer loves to research people on LinkedIn to find out where they went to school or other details to find points of connection.

"How are you today?" "How long have you been in Brooklyn?" Or even, "I love your dress! It's so flattering on you!" Or "You have great taste in brands. I love the way you merchandise your store!"

Try to avoid, 'How can I help you today? Are you looking for something in particular?' While those are innocent openers, most people don't really need help and even if they might be looking for something, they might not know what it is yet.

Remember, authentic compliments go a long way to develop rapport. Find a way to flatter or create a connection.

Ask questions and listen

No one wants to be talked *at, especially* people who are considering buying your products. Listen to your customers and ask more questions. You'd be surprised at how this helps you sell more.

Be human

Remember, people buy from people and they want to support your small business. Be relatable and be human.

Read body language (or tone)

Get comfortable and be aware of energy, body language, voice, and tone. You can tell when someone is opening up or closing down if you're mindful. Body language and energy start with you. Don't be attached to the outcome, and keep your energy positive instead of needy.

Be positive — even when your show sucks

Nothing is worse than trade or art show exhibitors complaining because the show is slow. Always act as if the show is your best ever. Get off your phone, stand in your booth, smile, and make eye contact with show attendees. You attract the energy you put out, so keep your vibe positive to attract customers.

Suggestive sell items

Once you have a captive audience or a customer ready to purchase, remember they don't really know your products as much as you do. Use the opportunity to "suggestive-sell" matching pieces or items that work well with the piece they're interested in buying. You can focus on best-sellers or items that coordinate for in person sales. Online, there are plenty of suggestive-selling applications that can be programmed with Shopify from Bold and other app developers. We'll have some listed at DesiredBrandEffect.com/resources.

Close the sale

There are many strategies to encourage people to buy and it's your job to authentically close the sale by being of service and giving them a reason to buy now. The "urgency close" is great when you're having a promotion because typically there are limited items available or special incentives are expiring. The "compliment close" is great to flatter someone, and after it's clear they are considering your pieces, say, "Can I wrap those up for you?" The "solutions-oriented" approach focuses on a problem the customer might be having. For instance, a woman is looking for a pair of earrings to wear on a date and she's trying on yours: "Those are so flattering on you! The blue color really brings out your eyes. If you want to get _____, those are the earrings!" I'm slightly exaggerating here, but you can see various ways to close a sale.

More than anything, sales confidence comes from practicing and discovering what works on the people who buy from you. Find your power pose and work on your closing skills to make more sales.

For more inspiration and sales training, listen to the Thrive by Design Podcast wherever you listen to podcasts or here at FlourishThriveAcademy .com/podcast.

Can't I Just Hire a Salesperson or Sales Representative?

Great question! I know that a majority of creatives reading this book would love to just outsource their sales. The answer is: someday, maybe. As I mentioned earlier, you will always be the best salesperson for your business. At some point, you might need or want to hire someone to support you at retail events, trade shows, in-house wholesale sales, or even to host your trunk shows; however, you can't expect this person to be the only revenue driver. That's why I always encourage you to take full accountability for your sales success by learning as much as you can about sales and doing it! That allows you to understand who your audience is and to what they are responding.

It's customary (not necessary) to have a sales rep or showroom once you've established your brand to maintain and grow your wholesale accounts. Keep in mind, paying a rep or showroom is expensive and most won't pick up a newer brand until they already have shown proof of concept—you are already in a bunch of stores and the stores are selling your products and reordering. I know from my students and my own experience that no one will ever sell as much as you. If you're thinking about hiring a salesperson, keep in mind that it will take time for them to grow, and there may not be sales immediately.

The best time to hire any sort of salesperson is when you can no longer keep up, you can afford to pay someone commission or a salary, and your attention is better focused elsewhere in the business.

Consistency and Persistence

I've seen a lot of brands become successful and a lot more that continue to struggle with selling, but what if you're doing everything in this book and still aren't getting consistent sales?

From mentoring over 7500+ designers through coaching, workshops, challenges, and programs, one of the biggest problems I see is a lack of commitment to consistency and follow-up from designers selling online and off. The result is slow or inconsistent sales. That makes them discouraged and actually perpetuates the problem. The best salespeople are consistent, persistent, and always focused on doing the actions that grow their business and serve their potential and current customers.

The other part of attracting Dream Clients goes back to understanding where they hang out (aka where to find them). For example, if you're trying to sell on TikTok or Snapchat, but your Dream Clients are 60 year-olds, more than likely you're not marketing and selling in the right place.

Or let's say your Dream Client is super outdoorsy, not into trends, loves nature, and does a lot of yoga. Where do you think that person would spend their time? Are they shopping in big brand department stores and going to high-end boutiques? Probably not. They might be going to artists' fairs, farmer's markets, coffee shops, and juice bars. Do your research and get clear on where they shop.

Same goes for selling into stores. Retail buyers are inundated with emails and calls from designers who are not a good fit for their store. That's why the best advice is always to do your research! Even if you don't sell to stores, understand the buying and lifestyle habits of your Dream Clients because this informs where you show up, market, sell, advertise, or even pitch the media. Again, do your research! Just because *you* love a store or a publication doesn't always mean your Dream Client is shopping there.

When deciding on a sales channel, get really clear where your prospective clients are shopping, not just where you want to sell your products. Show up on the social media platforms and blogs where your clients are hanging out online. Make sure your Dream Clients are the customers of the retail stores to which you pitch and sell. Walk every trade show before you invest to make sure it's the right place for your brand. Your marketing and sales efforts must be aligned with your Dream Client *first*.

Sales will come in when you can objectively evaluate where you're having success, get more consistent with that, and get into your flow. Consistency is not sending out an email newsletter once a month and putting a couple of posts on Instagram every week, but putting continual energy into growing your brand by testing and evaluating.

If you're in a place where you're striving to grow your sales, I invite you to check it out and look at some additional resources below. For now, suffice to say, becoming your best salesperson will get easier over time, particularly as your mindset shifts, your confidence grows, and your customer knowledge and sales targets become clearer. And nothing will help that more than if your marketing brings the right kinds of clients to your door.

Sales training is an ongoing evolution, so I encourage you to work on your sales mindset and come from a place of service. This section could be an entire book on its own! We have several programs at Flourish & Thrive Academy for emerging brands who would like help growing and scaling their sales. If you'd like to get some help growing your business, then I'd love to invite you to apply for a complimentary Strategy Audit with my team. During the audit, we'll take a look at your goals, vision for success and what's happening in your current business to help you design a clear path forward based on your unique situation. If you're interested in learning more, head on over to FlourishThriveAcademy.com/strategy.

CHAPTER 8

EXCEPTIONAL SERVICE

"The best way to tell if a brand is worth partnering with is after something goes wrong. How they handle it is everything."

— TARA SILBERBERG

Making a sale is not the end of your brand's relationship with your customers. Delivering a great brand experience before, during, and after the sale is key to the final stage of the Buyer Journey—loyalty. This is about keeping customers hooked on your brand and turning them into true fans who will stay with you throughout your brand's evolution. There's a saying in business, "If someone has a good experience, they'll tell their best friend. If someone has a bad experience, they'll tell *all* their friends."

Loyalty is not just a good thing as far as creating fans, but it's also a sound business strategy. It's much harder and more expensive to get a new customer to buy than to get an existing customer to buy again. Marketing, sales and promotions help you attract new clients. Exceptional customer service where you deliver great client experiences is how you keep them. When you do this well, you create lasting loyal true fans. Showing these people you care is the best investment you can make to grow your business over time. It's time to nurture those relationships.

Exceptional Service

Remember, your business is only as strong as the loyal customer base you have. While you think it might be all about designing pretty jewelry that people buy, it's more about creating a brand that is community- and customer-centric. Faceless brands are dying, so it's time to shift your perspective—you're not just selling jewelry, you're adding value to someone's life. When you deliver a great experience, a community of superfans form around your brand. Over time, this snowballs into organic growth and bigger reach.

Delivering a great experience starts long before the sale in your social interactions, your communication, and any touchpoint the customer has with your brand. It also happens long after the sale from how the product is packaged to what happens next. Will you follow up with your customers, or are you adopting a "ghosting" strategy where after they buy they never hear from you again? Create a post-purchase email sequence that is either automated or manual depending on the type of customer it is (i.e. wholesale vs. online vs. retail). The purpose is to take your customers on the next phase of their journey with your brand. Invite them to your community in a way that works for you, and acknowledge them with personal touches that go the extra mile. They'll remember you.

When I first started Flourish & Thrive Academy, I interviewed Tara Silberberg of The Claypot for a podcast series that I hosted. During that interview, she said something that really stood out to me: *"The best way to tell if a brand is worth partnering with [for the long run] is after something goes wrong. How they handle [a broken piece or difficult situation] is everything."* It doesn't matter if you're working with a store owner or a retail customer, what matters is how you handle the bad situations *and* the good situations. If you own a small business, you're in the customer service business. Always remember that. Your jewelry will break, it will be destroyed by careless wearers, and it will be frustrating to you. Remember, this is part of creating the Desired Brand Effect for your brand.

You've probably heard the old adage: the customer is always right. The point is not whether they are right or wrong. Sometimes the customer is wrong, and that's when service matters the most. It's your job to deliver exceptional service in all situations, and make your brand memorable for the right reasons, no matter what the situation.

What is Exceptional Service?

Exceptional service is your ability to surprise and delight your customers by creating a positive brand experience. You want to make it easy for customers to buy from you the first time and many times again. If you make it difficult for them to buy, they won't. Your goal, as a business owner, is to reduce the friction in the buying process and during any interaction with your brand so that you delight your customers and keep them loyal for life.

Today's consumers have many purchasing options, including competition on the internet, so brands must make it easy for customers to buy not just once, but over and over again. According to the Harvard Business Review, it costs six to seven times more to get a sale from a new customer than to get a sale from an existing one. A lot of designers feel like they need to "pound the pavement" to hunt down new customers. Perhaps that's true when you're getting started, but eventually you want the majority of your sales from repeat customers. That's why customer experience is so important to having healthy, growing sales!

Exceptional service is about exceeding your clients' expectations. Make "underpromise and overdeliver" your mantra. This could look like adding special touches such as handwritten thank-you notes or surprise gifts, shipping orders on time or early (with approval), helping wholesale accounts sell your products more quickly by creating trainings for their employees, simplifying how stockists reorder bestsellers, fixing or replacing damaged products quickly, offering ring maintenance on your custom engagement rings, and so on. These little extra touches inspire your clients to share their positive experience with everyone they know, eventually creating brand loyalty and encouraging the sharing economy.

DESIRED BRAND HIGHLIGHT: TRACY MATTHEWS

Throughout this book, I've featured many of my peers and students/mentees and shared their stories. For this example, I'd love to share with you how I created a multi-six-figure custom fine jewelry business by delivering an exceptional experience for my customers.

I met Quinn and his wife Jen* at my dear friend's wedding when Jen found out that I'm a jewelry designer. She was explaining how her husband (a successful investment banker) was terrible at buying her gifts. As she joked with the women about the thoughtless gifts Quinn's assistant had purchased her over the years, I could see that she was disappointed because she *really* wanted him to put some thought into the gifts he gave. The problem: he is clueless at gift buying and really needed help from someone who understands Jen.

Later, I side-barred with Quinn and told him I could

help. I made notes during my encounter with Quinn and Jen about key dates, style, tastes, and anything I could think of so that I could not only land them as a customer but design many pieces for Jen over time. They had the means, and she loved my jewelry. Over the course of several years, I helped Quinn surprise Jen with some incredible pieces of jewelry by making it really *easy* for him to buy from me. I reach out with a few ideas, he picks one, we make it and hand deliver it. To sweeten the experience, I offer regular jewelry maintenance for the items since many of them are worn frequently. One meeting on the beach led to a happy client who owns at least 15 of my fine jewelry designs over the years.

Communication

Creating a culture of exceptional service starts with communication. Nothing hurts your reputation more than a delayed response or unfriendly communication that isn't customer-focused. Make your customers feel heard (even if you think they're wrong) and lead with solutions instead of hashing out problems. This is why sales and customer service are so closely intertwined. Upleveling your communication includes the language you use, your frequency in communication, timeliness in response and how you approach and solve problems. If dealing with customers is not your forte or your business is too busy to deliver timely responses, do your business a favor and hire a customer service specialist or assign someone on your team the responsibility.

Language

Every company should define how it speaks to the outside world. Your brand voice and tone should resonate throughout all of your customer communications. Create messaging standards and scripts for email and phone communication that you can document and use over and over again. When emailing or speaking to customers, make sure you always outline the next steps. If you need a response from them, bullet out exactly what you need. Keep your emails short, concise and to the point. Remember, chatting on the phone can solve a variety of customer service problems in the long run.

Frequency and Timeliness

Your customer service responses should ideally be handled within 1-3 hours of the initial inquiry during your regular business hours. If you're doing everything yourself, do your best to respond while you have time blocked for emails. When you hire a customer service rep, create boundaries and a response time best practice. Think about how you'd like to be treated by others, and act that way. Don't go radio silent or you'll lose the customer forever. If you've reached out in a timely manner and you haven't gotten a response within a few days, follow up to make sure your message was received.

Solutions Focus

You are going to have issues and difficult customers. Products break, accidents happen, and some people are just hard to work with. Lead with the solution first, and don't use jargon or try to explain why something did or didn't happen. Simply fix the problem. If it's a repair, have a policy and for a period of time, fix the piece for no or minimal fee. These phrases can go a long way in establishing trust with your customers when something has gone wrong: "I'd be happy to help," "let me take care of that for you," and "I hear your frustration and I'd love to make it right."

Handling Difficult Situations

As I mentioned above, you are always going to encounter customer service problems in your business. Sometimes those problems get heightened and a customer might freak out or get angry. This might stress you out for a few reasons: the situation might cost significant money to fix, the customer might be wrong, or the customer might be rude or difficult.

In such situations, it's important that the customer feels heard. Approach all difficult situations by doing the following:

The Golden Rule

Treat others exactly as you'd like to be treated yourself! Put yourself in their shoes. You've heard the phrase: kill 'em with kindness. Be empathetic and kind even when it's challenging. How would you want a similar situation handled if you were the consumer? How would you feel or like to be treated when you're dealing with a difficult situation from a brand you've purchased from? Do the same for them!

Make them feel heard

One of the most challenging things to do in a crisis is to make the customer feel like they've been heard. Especially when you're starting out, any difficult situation might feel stressful. Regardless of the complaint, acknowledge their situation, grievance or feelings and offer a solution. There's no need to belabor the problem.

Go above and beyond

Have you ever encountered a situation where you were surprised at how well a company treated you? Create a plan to offer a special touch to accommodate a challenging situation. What can you do to go above and beyond the situation to make it right?

Deliver win-win solutions

No one ever wants to lose money or lose face in a difficult situation. Become solutions-oriented and deliver a resolution that is good for the customer first, but also good for you. For instance, if a wholesale customer isn't selling through on inventory, perhaps you swap it out for a new fresh product instead of losing the customer altogether.

Start with what you can do

Your customers don't want to hear about what you can't do. When you become solutions-oriented, you lead with phrases that impress upon the client how you can resolve this situation. Perhaps it's a replacement, fixing something that is broken, or changing the item for another version.

Ask for feedback on how to improve

After you've handled your delicate or difficult situation, ask the customer for feedback on how you can improve their experience. Oftentimes they might say you handled it well. However, you might also get invaluable feedback and hear something you never considered before. Keep an open mind.

Turning Disappointed Customers Into Raving Fans

Can you think back to a time when you received bad customer service? Maybe you needed to return something and lost the receipt and the customer service rep was giving you a hard time. Perhaps your flight got delayed and the airline attendant was super rude about you having to wait.

We've all had bad customer service experiences. In your business, make certain that no customer ever does. Anytime someone has a complaint or problem, go above and beyond to make it right. Get on the phone with them, listen to them, tell them you understand and take full responsibility for anything that is yours. And, finally, offer a solution or invite them to help create the solution. This puts them in the position of power, which is really all they want.

Sometimes you can turn a misunderstanding or a complaint into another sale. Once, a friend of mine bought a ring online from a cool new designer she discovered. When it arrived, she loved it and wore it the next day. By the end of the day, the gold had worn off and her finger was green. She emailed the designer saying how sad she was that this happened because she really loved the ring and was hoping it was higher quality. She didn't even ask for a refund. She just explained how bummed out she was and asked to buy a replacement with higher quality materials. This designer responded immediately and told her she would send her a ring with upgraded materials at no cost! When it arrived, there was a hand-written note apologizing and hoping she enjoyed this new ring. My friend was so blown away that she posted a picture of the note and ring on her Instagram account saying how wonderful the designer handled the situation. She recommended all her friends check out this brand.

This is a perfect example of how you can turn a negative experience into a positive one for your customers! You want people to stick with you not only because they love your jewelry, but because they know you care about them.

DESIRED BRAND HIGHLIGHT:
KATE SYDNEY JEWELRY

Kate Sydney was selling on a third-party platform many years ago before she had her branded website set up. While the sales weren't phenomenal, she would occasionally get orders. One day, she saw a return request for a piece she'd sold. The customer was complaining about a "natural inclusion" in the watermelon tourmaline stone. Kate wanted to save the sale so she reached out to the third-party platform (not Etsy) and begged for the email address of the customer. Eventually, they agreed.

After reaching out to the customer and apologizing profusely for the disappointment, Kate explained her process for sourcing only natural stones and agreed to replace the stone with one of the customer's liking. The customer was so pleased that Kate reached out to her that she repurchased the original piece and added four more pieces to her original order.

Kate realized she had a huge opportunity to make more and better sales on her website, so she followed the strategy we teach in our Momentum program to build her email list, set up email sequences that nurture prospects and sell on autopilot, and send our regular broadcast emails to her list.

After leaning into this strategy and getting consistent with follow-up, Kate noticed that the formerly disappointed customer had purchased five pieces for her next OOAK collection release. Kate reached out to the customer to thank her with a personal message, then when she saw the customer purchased at the next launch, she began sending hand-written thank you notes.

Now, each time Kate launches a new collection, this same customer buys five to seven pieces. Even with an average price point of $185 a piece, she sold over $8500 worth of jewelry in one year to this customer just by showing up and delivering, turning a bad situation around, and creating an exceptional customer experience.

The Tools of Exceptional Service

Difficult situations will always arise in your business. The more tools you have to handle them with grace and ease, the better the experience for your customers. When a customer feels seen and heard, and you deliver a win-win solution, you are gaining a customer for life.

Information is your friend, which is why tools are especially valuable. If something goes wrong, an order gets lost or your shipping date gets pushed back, you need a record of it so you can make things right. People understand things go wrong, but when they feel like you're making them a priority, they're less likely to get upset.

FAQs and canned responses

The easiest way to deal with customer service issues is to develop a knowledge base of Frequently Asked Questions that you can pull from on a regular basis. Your FAQs should be centered around your policies and the questions people ask you often. As questions come up, craft your answer and then add it to your FAQs document. You can post a version of this document as a page on your website and keep it in your customer service SOP as canned responses.

No one wants to be sent to an FAQs page on your website for a cookie-cutter answer. Even if you have that FAQ page complete with every answer to every question possible, send your customers a personalized response when they reach out. You can have most of the response pre-written and add one sentence acknowledging their unique situation.

Policies, terms and conditions

To overcome the stress of difficult situations, make sure you have standard terms and conditions and policies. You should have a shopping cart terms and conditions, a privacy policy and a general terms of use policy for your website. While the policies might vary for wholesale vs. retail customers, your terms and conditions should cover returns, repairs, damages, payments, sale or return (if you have this), shipping windows, and anything else that might come up. That way there's no question when something goes wrong.

Tech

One of the best ways to create a better experience of your brand for your customer is to use technology. Systems that increase your ability to help your customers and smooth the nurturing and buying process are great for developing trust and getting repeat sales. This results in Scaling Desire, which we will talk about later in the book, but for now you can think of it simply as taking care of your customers.

Depending on your business, this might include:

- ◆ Automated email sequences to deliver pre- and post-purchase experiences
- ◆ Live chat or messaging on your site
- ◆ A contact form and phone number on your website (use a Google voice number if you don't have a dedicated work number)
- ◆ A customer service CRM application like Zendesk or Intercomm to improve their experience
- ◆ A CRM tool like HubSpot or Insightly for managing manual customer interactions

It's important to have a good CRM so that you can manage, organize, and analyze all your customer interactions throughout the entire lifecycle. This helps you remember who you're supposed to follow up with and when. Having a system keeps you focused on the customer relationships rather than sales numbers, because of the kind of information you can see.

Together, these tools can help you get to know your customers so that you can create opportunities to make them feel extra special.

Wash, rinse and repeat customer service experiences
The best way to give each customer and client a good buying experience is by setting up a system. It may feel less authentic or personalized to you when you start to automate. In fact, automation can feel like an icky word, but it can be done in a way that still feels tailored and caring for your clients.

You can't have a 1:1 personal conversation with every single client, every single time. Eventually, something is bound to fall through the cracks, and when it does, you'll end up doing your clients a disservice by missing a step or forgetting to follow up. We all forget things from time to time. This is why brands need systems for the entire customer lifecycle. In Chapter 11, we will cover systems and automation in more detail, so that you can provide smooth and consistent customer experience while growing your sales.

Surprise and Delight
It's not just when things go wrong that you have opportunities to provide exceptional service. Customer experience is so important to having healthy, growing sales through loyalty and repeat business. Whenever possible, *exceed* your clients' expectations and you'll eventually create brand advocates. Customers can make some of your best sales reps if you surprise and delight them.

When you know your clients, listen to their needs, follow up with them, and focus on helping them out, sales come naturally. Find little ways to go above and beyond. For your wholesale accounts, meet in person with buyers so you're not just another designer. Send your clients thank-you notes, birthday cards, and special gifts. Respond quickly to messages and always do what you say you're going to do. Create community around your brand by acknowledging your superfans publicly. These simple gestures help them feel understood and appreciated.

At the end of the day, your business has a reputation that starts and ends with your ability to deliver an exceptional customer experience. When you do this right, repeat sales are easy to attract. Your happy customers become your best source of referrals, and growing your sales becomes super easy!

CHAPTER 9

REVENUE-GENERATING ACTIVITIES

"Talent is less important than the actions you take on a daily basis that support your dreams."
— TRACY MATTHEWS

Have you ever sat down to work on your business and realized you don't actually know what you should be doing each day in order to reach your goals? You might even feel super busy all of the time, but you end the day feeling frustrated because you didn't get enough done. Perhaps you're working harder than ever and still not seeing the results you desire. I think we've all been here at one point or another. It's completely overwhelming and demotivating to feel like you're working hard and not growing!

If you're constantly scraping by financially, you're probably not focusing your time on the right activities. The purpose of this chapter is to help you identify how to spend your time to reach your sales goals so you can get off the treadmill of constant busy work and get into flow with the work that really matters as a leader of your business.

Activities that Generate Revenue

Revenue-generating activities (RGAs) are defined as any activity that gets your brand exposure, makes sales, generates leads, or attracts potential prospects. RGAs encompass pretty much any active marketing or sales activity, including but not limited to making sales calls, writing emails, developing marketing campaigns, and pitching PR and exposure opportunities.

The number one reason that artists and makers get stuck in feast or famine mode is they lack focus on RGAs. I understand why—If you don't have sales momentum, it's hard to put yourself out there. Growing a successful jewelry company is part mindset, part talent, and part action taken on a daily basis to reach your goals. It's not enough to just dream or set a goal, you have to support that goal with actions.

Consistent revenue-generating activities will bring steady exposure and sales. If you're getting derailed, distracted, or pulled into the day-to-day of your business, you might feel like blowing RGAs off. Sadly, you might see the symptom of that as it translates into profit plateau or slow sales. Your success as a business owner relies on spending the majority of your focus on RGAs to create predictable, repeat sales and profitable revenue streams.

Since we are all unique individuals with unique brands, the way we build our businesses will vary. However, the *types* of actions we take will be similar. The common activities that most creative products brands will need to focus on are:

- Sales calls
- Emails
- Marketing campaigns
- Pitching PR
- Collaboration and exposure opportunities
- Consistent outreach

- ◆ E-commerce strategy and implementation
- ◆ Promotions
- ◆ Digital marketing
- ◆ Product development
- ◆ Audience nurturing
- ◆ Diversifying your revenue streams

When you pinpoint the right RGAs for your business and begin investing enough time in them, your sales will grow and become more predictable. If you don't, you're at risk of perpetuating a cycle of inconsistent sales.

Since RGAs vary depending on the structure and nature of your brand, develop yours around your business model and revenue streams. Figuring out which RGAs to focus on first begins with developing your 90-day strategic plan and being clear on your goals. We'll cover strategic planning fully in Chapter 10. That plan then gets broken down into specific strategies and tactics that back up the strategy for achieving your 90-day plan. If the terms strategy and tactics seem the same to you, think of strategies as high-level, big-picture goals that encompass the overarching project. Tactics are the tasks that support the bigger strategy, promotion, or project—your RGAs!

So that you can decide what your most effective RGAs or tactics will be, let's take a look at what you could be doing to move your business forward. To recap, RGAs for a direct-to-consumer may include:

- ◆ Building your email list
- ◆ Emailing your list
- ◆ Hosting a virtual trunk show
- ◆ Creating an abandoned cart sequence
- ◆ Running retargeting ads
- ◆ Optimizing website for conversions
- ◆ Testing sms marketing

- ◆ Optimizing for search engines
- ◆ Executing creating a social media plan and posting daily

RGAs for a wholesale strategy include:

- ◆ Following up with existing accounts for re-order
- ◆ Emailing prospective accounts weekly
- ◆ Researching and applying for tradeshows
- ◆ Following up with your busiest accounts
- ◆ Following up with orders once they've been shipped

Each of the tactics above can be designed into your high-performance plan based on priorities. Imagine how productive you will be if you start each and every day focused specifically on the activities you *know* are going to grow your brand and bring in money.

How Much of This Do You Need to Do?

Discovering and scheduling the right RGAs for your business will boost your sales and keep you on a growth trajectory. I recommend spending 75% of your time on activities that bring money into your business. No matter what phase of business you're in, if you're taking this seriously and committed to growth and success, you will need to focus on RGAs for the majority of your time.

When I started my first business, I spent most of my time on tasks that weren't bringing in money. This was an excuse to avoid what I needed to do to get my business going: driving sales. Many creative entrepreneurs become stuck in perfectionism prison where they try to make everything perfect before they put it out there. Yep, that was me, and I realize now being a perfectionist was just a fear of rejection in disguise. I didn't want people to say no to me, but eventually I knew something had to shift.

For me, that came in the form of the ultimatum my then-husband gave me that day he came home and said: "Tracy, you have to make sales or go back to your retail job!" I knew he was right. I'd been stuck in perfectionism prison for six months and needed to get my work out there. That all started with my changing my mindset. (In Chapter 7, we covered in some detail how to reframe your relationship with sales.) From there, every day, I would make a list of at least three priorities (RGAs) to move my business forward. And I didn't allow myself to do anything else until those RGAs were completed.

Little by little, I built momentum by focusing more on my RGAs. Before I knew it, I'd made over $50,000 in revenue in my first year. I doubled down on the amount of time I spent on RGAs. By the time I was spending 75% of my working hours on my RGAs in my second year, I made $150,000 in revenue. I've used the same philosophy over the past 25 years to grow several multi six- and seven-figure companies and have taught thousands of my students and mentees to do the same for their businesses. This can happen for you, too, if you spend most of your time moving your business forward and dialing in on the activities that bring money into your business.

When you focus on your RGAs for 75% of your time, you may begin to realize how much time you're wasting on things that don't really matter for your growth, especially stressing about being rejected or just handling a to-do list that probably could be thrown in the wastebin. Instead, you might consider that there are more important questions to ask yourself, like: Why aren't these pieces selling? Am I getting my designs in front of my Dream Clients? Who can I partner with to expand my audience? Why aren't my wholesale stores reordering my new collection? I am no stranger to rejection—and this line of thinking will move you into proactive and problem solving mode. Think of rejection as constructive feedback and continue to move forward.

As Chief Visionary Officer of your business, focusing on the highly leveraged activities that will grow your sales (aka your RGAs) is essential. That's how you create traction and move forward. Not all creators and makers apply the 75% rule, but the ones who spend their time primarily on their RGAs—and make them non-negotiable—are the ones who see the most success. If you treat your RGAs as optional and fail to organize your days and weeks around these activities, they won't happen. It's easy to tell yourself that you'll find the time to do them if you put them on your to-do list, but we all know that's not true. We will find every reason to procrastinate on tasks that make us uncomfortable, which makes them that much easier to put off.

While 75% of your time may sound like a lot, let's be real. If your business isn't bringing in revenue, you don't really have a business. Changing your weekly actions and daily habits is the only way you'll change your results. What does it look like to focus on RGAs on a weekly and daily basis? How does working towards revenue generation fit with your overall marketing plan? And how can you create a workflow that keeps you focused on revenue-generating activities that make your business succeed? Let's take a look at productivity.

RGAs and Productivity

Focusing on RGAs really works to get you to the next level, no matter how long you've been in business. The Desired Brand Effect methodology is deliberately designed to address this exact problem, because the pillars center on revenue generation, brand exposure, connected conversion and scaling.

RGAs are the life-blood of your business and they deserve the majority of your time, which means consistent daily and weekly focus, not sporadic or occasional attention. Starting each week without a plan will be detrimental to your impact and growth. If you don't know where you're going or how to get there, how will you ever reach your destination?

Former CEO of Alex and Ani jewelry illustrated the power of planning and its impact on productivity when he shared with a member of our community how his company went from $4 million to $250+ million in just four years, which is an insane growth trajectory, even for a seven-figure company. He put his success down to rigorous focus on revenue-generating activities. Every single day, the first block of his time before noon was spent working on business development—no phone, no text, no email that was not directly related to achieving the ambitious goals set out for the company. He scheduled his day to focus on the most important activities that he needed to complete first and then moved on to less important tasks.

DESIRED BRAND HIGHLIGHT:
LAURA MICHAEL OF
A WORTHY BRAND

When Laura Michael launched her brand, she went all in for her dream to have a six-figure lifestyle business. When she came to us for support, she only had an idea for a jewelry company that empowered women to feel worthy and love themselves. Slowly but surely, she followed the steps in the Desired Brand Effect and made RGAs a priority every day.

Her strategy was to build a multi-stream business first by focusing on one revenue stream at a time. She sells on her branded website, Etsy, Amazon Handmade, and wholesale. By dialing in one sales channel at a time, her business took off. Instead of spreading herself too thin, she created an RGA flow for each channel and a system for growth. She started having one sale a day, which then snowballed into 750+ sales a month. Within two years of starting her jewelry business A Worthy Brand, she hit her six-figure goal and continues to grow now. Laura attributes her success to being consistent and continuing on even when it gets hard.

If you say you want success but approach your days, weeks, and months blindly, you'll always be struggling to catch up and likely see your profits plateau. The symptom is almost always the dreaded feeling of spinning your wheels. The solution to feeling overwhelmed is structure—yes, creatives thrive in structure even if you don't think it's for you. That structure is derived from your 90-day strategic plan that is broken down into tangible projects, goals, and weekly deliverables. You've heard the saying: How do you eat an elephant? One bite at a time! Same thing here.

Here's what structure looks like on a weekly basis:

- Weekly scheduling
- Daily priorities
- Time-blocking

Starting your week with a plan is a business game-changer, but it must be strategic and tie into bigger-picture goals. Although it might seem obvious to some, I'm continually surprised by how many people don't know what they're trying to accomplish in their business. Nor do they have weekly tasks to reach those goals. Everything you're holding yourself accountable for day-to-day and week-to-week comes from your 90-day strategic plan, so make sure you're using this as a roadmap to break out your weekly tasks, then daily tasks, then time-blocking.

Once you know that your RGAs should be based on your broader strategy, you can break them down into weekly and daily priorities to keep you motivated and on point. In Chapter 10, I'll go into detail on how to do this higher-level planning. For now, let's look at weekly scheduling.

Weekly plan and schedule

You are a creative being and your creative thinking is the one thing that will continually grow your business for the long haul. However, you need to protect that creative energy like a warrior. You'll do that by adding more structure, not less, into your days and weeks.

The method I prefer is to designate different theme days and time-block each day so that you know exactly what you're working on and when. Ideally, you'll schedule certain types of activities together. For instance, Mondays and Wednesdays are PR and marketing days, Tuesdays and Thursdays are sales and call days, and Fridays are creative days. This is a broad generalization. Realistically, most days may be slated for multiple objectives. The key point is that you know exactly what you're focusing on in any given week on any given day.

Here's an example of how I structure my week:

- ◆ **Monday:** morning planning, content, and podcast recording
- ◆ **Tuesday:** meetings and marketing strategy
- ◆ **Wednesday:** creative days for design or completion of big projects
- ◆ **Thursday:** meetings and leadership focus
- ◆ **Friday:** finishing up loose ends and ideation

How might you break up your week so that you consistently work on your goals?

Daily prioritizing and time-blocking

Creativity needs space. If you're trying to squish creative content, design, or making time in-between meetings, you'll likely get into your creative zone, then have to "context-switch," which is highly unproductive. When you do this often, you probably feel frazzled and like you didn't get much done. The magic of time-blocking is that your brain will thrive when it knows exactly what it's supposed to be working on in advance because you set an appointment for yourself on your calendar.

Batches of content creation or working on sales initiatives can be completed in larger time blocks. Calls or repetitive admin tasks can be scheduled in hour-long appointment blocks in your calendar. The more dedicated the time blocks in your day, the more you will get done. Powerful results will follow when you find your own rhythm and flow around *your* most productive time during the day. You'll also want to check in at the beginning of each day to adjust your plan and confirm your schedule.

A designer in our Momentum coaching program worked with our coaches to time block her days—that year she doubled her sales *and* eliminated the paper explosion on her desk by moving everything to her calendar. Another designer mentioned that time-blocking helped her grow her side hustle design business to high four figures a month while she was working a full-time job.

While you may be scheduling your week and blocking your time, all of this is for nothing if you're not focusing on the right things in your business. That means setting goals and achieving them. This topic is so important to me, because I've seen so many talented designers focusing on the wrong activities, not seeing any growth, then giving up. This is heartbreaking, because even with all the talent in the world, what makes someone successful are the actions they put in to move their business forward.

As a result, it's important to also set daily priorities so that your *most important* (not the most urgent or easiest or most fun) work gets done during your most productive hours each day. It's human nature to go for the easy tasks first, but this only distracts you from the most important tasks that move the needle in your business. Select three top priorities per day and work on those when you have the most energy, making sure you don't move on to anything else until they're finished.

Regular creative days

Creative founders *need* to be creative often if they want to have successful businesses, but creativity is not just making your products. Creativity is also ideation, strategy, new product design, and business development. Creative thinking time is the most important asset that you have in business, so if you're spending most of your time making your art instead of creatively growing your business, you're doing yourself and your business a disservice.

The key to finding the time to "think" is by scheduling out creative days for business development and strategy. At first, you may feel like you don't know what to do on those days, and you might feel like you're floundering. Get clear on where you're going first and then use this time to create the strategy. You'll also notice how you can marry your creativity with business development, and maybe even feel happier because

212   *Revenue-Generating Activities*

you'll start exploring all those wonderful ideas that you normally can't find time for.

Creative days are great for designing new collections, coming up with high-level business strategy, content creation, learning something new, and working on big projects. They should not be used for production, repetitive tasks, or checking boxes off your list. If you're ready to try out creative days for yourself, start with just one day a month and gradually increase that to one day a week. Get in your flow. You started a creative business for a reason!

Boundaries

In this digital world, there are distractions everywhere: notifications on your phone, calendar events, social media, texts, phone, email, people around you. You need to protect your energy and set boundaries. If you don't, you'll always feel overwhelmed and pulled in so many directions. I get at least 20 messages a week to my personal Instagram handle and at least 20 messages or more a day on the Flourish & Thrive Academy account. I can always tell when a designer in our community is leaking energy and not setting boundaries, because I'll message them and right away I see the dots pop up that they are writing back.

When I started my first business, many of my team members worked in my office, and I struggled to set boundaries because I didn't know much about leadership. All day every day, I'd be interrupted by people asking me questions. I thought I was supposed to have an open-door policy, but I quickly realized that my energy was completely drained by the end of the day. I was doing pretty much everything, because my team was using my brain instead of their own.

The lack of boundaries resulted in a team that could not problem-solve. To work toward a more productive environment, I started implementing office hours. If my team had questions, they could only ask during the three 30-minute windows that I created. Also, they had to come to me with three possible solutions to their problem and together we'd decide on the right move or collaborate if their ideas weren't in line with our objectives. The result? I got a lot more done, I was more energized and I became a better boss. Our sales scaled and the team had fewer questions, because they weren't reliant on me and they grew into independent thinkers.

Protecting your time and energy is key. Do this by turning off notifications and sounds on your phone and email. Schedule time to respond to texts, emails, and social media comments and direct messages. Organize your work space so you're more productive. Get enough sleep and stop working right up till bedtime.

If you're not convinced that scheduling will work for you, I challenge you to just try it for one or two weeks: schedule your week, prioritize your top three daily tasks, time-block your day and turn off distractions. Then just see how much you get done!

Productivity tools

Some of us try to keep everything in our heads instead of using tools that can help free up energy and make us more productive. If you don't know where to start or which tools to use, you're even more inclined to stick with a manual process. However, if you want to maximize your productivity and set yourself up for success, try using tools and software developed to help you succeed.

You can find applications or software to track sales and inventory, manage email and projects, streamline communication, and create shortcuts so you don't have to think about it. Using tools such as CRMs and project management platforms will help you keep your ideas sorted and your business scaling for the long term. If you want to stop feeling so overwhelmed all the time, integrate one tool at a time to help increase your performance and impact. The ultimate goal in all of this is to increase your productivity while streamlining all of the activities that bring more money into your business.

Here are just a few productivity tools that we recommend in our programs that you can start playing with for yourself:

Zapier — A productivity tool that seamlessly connects all your business apps like Gmail, Slack and Klaviyo. Zapier can automate routine tasks that you do on a regular basis.

Slack — A place to keep team communications streamlined and organized. Different channels can be created for different projects or groups, and team members can jump in and out of conversations as needed, instead of getting emails or notifications that are not relevant to them.

Trello or Asana — Project management tools that make planning and managing projects simple by breaking big projects into smaller chunks and arranging those in order of completion.

Todoist — A to-do list app that helps to categorize and schedule tasks on your to-do list. The software interprets and categorizes the tasks for you based on your entries.

Social media planners — Using s social media content scheduler or planner for Facebook, Twitter, Instagram, YouTube, Pinterest, and LinkedIn allows you to access multiple platforms without having to log into each one separately.

Togl — A time-tracker app that allows you to have folders for different tasks or projects, and create detailed reports for billing. Perfect for keeping track of freelancers and contractors.

Brain.fm — A focus app that helps you get things done and uses brain research to create functional, purpose-driven music to put your brain into a desired state for productivity.

DESIRED BRAND HIGHLIGHT:
KATY BEH

Katy Beh is a single mom and a designer who worked with us to implement the Desired Brand Effect in her business. As a goldsmith who loves the process of making more than anything, overcoming the mental hurdles to keep putting herself out there was challenging at first. Katy has amazing talent so there is no reason why she shouldn't reach her goal of $150,000 by the end of the year, but it was becoming a mental game.

During the time Katy worked with us, she shifted her focus to only doing what was bringing her powerful results and positioned her brand as the go-to jeweler in New Orleans. In particular, she leveraged her in-person shows like Jazz Fest to build her local customer base. When she compared her first quarter against the previous year, she had grown 72%, and by the end of the year, she had hit her $150,000 goal.

By implementing systems and support in her business, Katy could focus on her RGAs without feeling overwhelmed by everything else. A lot of these changes came from spending more time on relationship development and follow-up strategies for events, as well as streamlining her workflow so she can do what she loves most.

Experiment!

In the beginning, you might have to try some things out and see what really works for your business model. Being consistent is truly the biggest battle. Once you find a strategy that works best for you, you'll be amazed at how quickly your income can increase.

An important note on experimenting with RGAs. The fortune is in the follow-up. Don't try something once then give up and move on to something else. Now more than ever, people are *busy*. Even when you have every intention of doing something, it can get pushed back a few weeks without even realizing it. The same is true for your clients and customers. It may feel like they're saying no, when really they mean not now. Building a sustainable jewelry business takes time. Your success depends on perseverance and patience. Great salespeople are resilient. Don't get down on yourself when someone turns you down. Remember, for every nine no's you get, you'll likely make a sale.

While you develop your RGA practice, keep this in mind. Perseverance creates momentum and a snowball effect over time. With that being said, relationship-building takes time, sometimes years for wholesale accounts, so if your results come slowly at first, that's normal. Stay focused on your RGAs and set time-based goals for outreach and sales. Even if you don't hit the goals right away, you're moving closer to them, and that's still growth.

PART THREE:

SCALING DESIRE

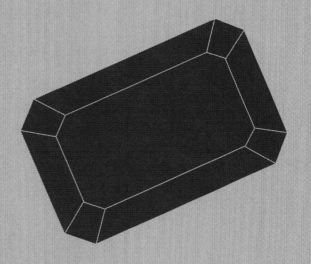

CHAPTER 10

STRATEGIC BUSINESS PLANNING

"Our goals can only be reached through the vehicle of a plan. There is no other route to success."
— PABLO PICASSO

G oals are achieved by having a crystal-clear vision of where you're going, then creating a plan to get there. Your vision guides the direction of your business and it's just as important as creating the strategic plan. Without it, your business will stagnate.

One of the biggest mistakes I see ambitious designers making is that they don't take the appropriate time to create a strategic plan that supports their big-picture vision. Instead, they end up building their business blindly with unfocused action and little direction. They get completely overwhelmed or frustrated because they aren't growing and they don't know why.

You might be thinking: *Tracy, I've built a business for the past X years without planning, and I've got this far.* Yes, there are some unicorns who may have seen growth without proper visioning and planning. However, those people have a tendency to burn out; it's extremely challenging to sustain long-term without goals and financial targets.

The Business Planning You Actually Need

The truth is planning for your business doesn't have to take a lot of time. In fact, the *last* thing I think any creative visionary should do is to create an extensive "old school" business plan. In 1998, I made the huge mistake of doing this and it cost me so much time that I didn't have. Every night and all weekend for three months, I'd pull out my 3-inch thick Dell Laptop and start typing into my business planning software. When it was done, it was a 30-page document that was full of arbitrary sales projections, my fantasy salary, and some generic market research that was completely unhelpful. You know what I did with that 30-page business plan? I shoved it in a filing cabinet and never looked at it again. I will never get that time back. However, I did learn an invaluable lesson back then: Yes, I needed a plan ... but it didn't need to be 30 pages.

So, let's talk about what that planning actually looks like for your business.

There are three types of plans that you need to make:

◆ A three-year vision
◆ A one-page business plan
◆ A 90-day strategic plan

Here's what these mean. The vision sets out where you're going in your business, the one-page business plan covers key targets like sales and growth projections, and the 90-day strategic plan encompasses how you'll reach the goals you created in the business plan.

Creating a Three-Year Vision

Creating a vision of where you want to go is a powerful exercise in manifesting what you desire in your business and in your life. It's important to think about both life and business because you might create a business that runs your life instead of creating a life that supports your business. I recommend casting a vision for the next three years and keeping that vision in mind as you create your business plan.

Your three-year vision is slightly different from the vision statement we talked about in Chapter 5. A company's vision statement is typically a short and concise sentence or paragraph. For instance, the vision statement for Flourish & Thrive Academy is:

To empower designers/makers to create financial security for themselves by doing what they love through our world class coaching and education programs.

Our three-year vision is quite different. It's a five-page document that covers not only the impact we make, but the goals of the company and the people we serve. So, take the concise vision statement of where you are going, and add to it the impact you want to make, your revenue targets, and anything else that sets you apart as an industry leader. Your three-year vision would also incorporate who you want to be as an entrepreneur and your personal and life goals, which is why I call it an aligned vision.

It includes:

◆ your role in the company
◆ the impact you are making as a designer
◆ how the external world sees your brand
◆ how you're being featured in the media
◆ the revenue your company is making
◆ the audience you serve
◆ your why and your core values
◆ what your brand stands for
◆ what your personal life looks like outside of work

This last one is very important, because there is no point in creating a business that does not support the life you want to lead. That's unsustainable and the fast track to burnout.

In his book *Vivid Vision*, Cameron Herold says that creating a Vivid Vision brings the future into the present. Sharing it with others makes the vision a reality, so you'll communicate it out into the world, to your team, and to your audience on a regular basis.

Your three-year vision is the guidepost for where you're going as a company and that means all of your other planning supports that vision. Your vision statement is you claiming what you'd like to create in the future. Your business plan maps out how you'll do this.

Proper Business Planning

Do you have a roadmap to reach where you'd like to go? If not, it's time to consider making one. If you don't know where you're going, it will be really hard to achieve anything. Imagine trying to drive across the country (or in my case, to the grocery store) without a map or any directions. You might eventually end up where you want to go, but you're likely going to take a lot of detours along the way.

In business, taking detours equates to lost time, money, and opportunities. This part of your brand journey might not feel as exciting as the other parts, but it's essential to your long-term success. Now that you've created a big-picture vision for your business, it's time to dial that into an actionable plan. You will need to center your plan around *growth* to include financial targets (like profit margins) and sales goals in addition to the other initiatives you're moving forward as a company.

As I mentioned before, you do not need a complicated business plan. In fact, your business plan can be a single page. A great tool to create this is a book by Jim Horan called the *One-Page Business Plan*. Your one-page business plan can include:

- your mission statement and core values
- your three-year vision
- your objectives and goals for the year

As a reminder, your mission statement is a short one-liner that dials in what your business aims to achieve, and your core values are a guidepost on what you stand for. These may refine and evolve over time, but generally tend to stay the same year after year.

Every year, you can list out the major goals you have as a designer. So that they are achievable, your goals should be SMART goals, meaning they are:

- **S**pecific
- **M**easurable
- **A**chievable
- **R**ealistic
- **T**ime-based

Making a **s**pecific goal means you write exactly who, what and even why you are setting the goal. Ask questions like who needs to be involved and when is the best time to deliver a campaign, and describe in detail what you are looking to achieve. Your goals should have metrics and exact numbers attached to them (**m**easurable). Ensure that those numbers are based on some real information of what you think you can do (**a**chievable) and that you have the means to make them happen (**r**ealistic). Keeping it **t**ime-bound means that you don't keep pushing the timeline back. Having a precise date or rough deadline keeps you accountable and is really important for being able to say whether you did or didn't hit your goal.

Take a look at these examples and see how they are all written with the SMART framework in mind:

◆ *Increase the overall company revenue from $90,000 to $150,000 by year-end*

◆ *Increase direct-to-consumer online sales revenue from our own website from $5,000 a month to $10,000 a month by August 31st*

◆ *Get 30% of my Etsy customer sales to sign up for my email list*

◆ *Build the email list from 1000 subscribers to 2500 subscribers by December 31st*

◆ *Increase my wholesale accounts from 20 stores to 40 stores by October 31st*

◆ *Hire a part-time Marketing and Sales Assistant by May 31st*

◆ *Land two media placements per month for the year*

◆ *Launch a spring collection by February 28th*

◆ *Launch a holiday collection by July 31st*

◆ *Improve overall profit margins by 10% by year end*

◆ *Grow Instagram following by 200 followers a month*

Think of your business plan as the annual overview version of your planning. Keep it to one page and go into the details of your core initiatives in your 90-day strategic plans. Wondering how you'll reach these goals or targets? That's where your strategic plan comes into play.

Strategies to Reach Your Goals

Before we get into your 90-day strategic plan, let's look at some examples of strategies more broadly, because it's a word that can mean different things to different people and often gets overcomplicated. Strategies are simply a thoughtful approach with a targeted outcome. Here are some examples so that you can see what I mean:

◆ *Focus on an owned marketing strategy to increase our email list size and traffic to the website*

◆ *Develop an expanded outreach strategy for wholesale accounts*
◆ *Map out collection and sample development timelines two months in advance of completion of the collections*
◆ *Document the marketing process and expectations so that I can train a Marketing Assistant*
◆ *Improve quality control standards to improve customers satisfaction*
◆ *Create an ambassador program to grow social following and website sales*

These strategies are broad and are supported by your 90-day strategic plan and an action plan.

Creating a 90-Day Strategic Plan

Now that you have an annual plan, it's time to turn that vision into a reality. Your 90-day strategic plan is designed to allow you to be flexible and pivot based on what's in front of you while helping you stay on track to your bigger goals. Think of your 90-day strategic plan as your Google Maps to the top. The destination is the same, but you can get there via lots of different routes. Your 90-day strategic plan will become the directions you need to reach that destination and achieve your vision of success. It is one of the first steps in removing yourself to scale your business, preparing you for Scaling Desire, which we cover in Part 3.

Even though you might not know this yet, you want to build a business that does not just require you to grow but also allows you to thrive. Strategies are the starting point. As you develop your strategies, you'll support them with action steps.

Just like it sounds, you create a 90-day strategic plan every quarter. Your plan should include the top three initiatives you have for the quarter and the detailed action steps of how you'll get there. Your 90-day strategic plan will include:

- ◆ a reminder of your vision
- ◆ a theme that guides your quarterly activity in one-to-three words
- ◆ core initiatives with goals and action steps for each

Goals

To inspire growth, you can set tiered goals with your revenue targets, which might include a must-have, nice-to-have, and stretch goal. Your must-have goal is the absolute must to make this initiative go off without a hitch. Your nice-to-have goal is your opportunity to push yourself a little beyond what you think you can do. Your stretch goal is a knock it out of the park goal that gets you super excited.

Actions

Next, you'll detail the actual tactics that it will take for you to reach your goals. This is your action plan. You can list some broad tactics on your annual business plan, but where you dial into the nitty gritty is in your 90-day strategic plan. It's hard for the mind not to be overwhelmed by taking it one year at a time. That's why we want to turn these big goals into smaller actionable plans.

Based on your annual business plan, take your top three initiatives per quarter and map them out onto your 90-day strategic plan. I encourage you to focus on no more than three big projects per quarter. You can always get ahead and start a new project if you complete the three projects ahead of time.

While you will likely go into more depth in your project management system, specifying the tasks and subtasks for each project, the example below shares an overview of how to break down those three core quarterly initiatives.

In the beginning, this process might feel a little daunting, but think about how empowered you're going to feel when you have a strong handle on what needs to happen to reach your goals. A clear plan gives you the freedom and ability to scale. It allows you to stop spending time on low-leveraged activities with little financial reward, and begin delegating so you can elevate your brand. With a clear and well-executed plan, you get your nights and weekends back! Not to mention your creativity, since you'll free up space to work on the parts of your business you love.

General action steps might look like:

- *Develop a weekly email marketing strategy and start sending out three emails a week by March 15th*
- *Develop ride-along inserts for shipments to grow email list for third party sales (Etsy etc) by February 28th*
- *Develop a PR hit list and send out 10 PR pitches a week (ongoing)*
- *Develop a dream wholesale store list by April 15th and sign up for a wholesale portal by June 30th*
- *Commit to five wholesale outreach a week (ongoing)*
- *Create a hiring funnel to source an ideal marketing assistant candidate by April 30th*
- *Commit to developing five systems a week so that I can train and delegate marketing (ongoing)*
- *Set up email automation for abandoned carts, nurture, and list cleanse campaign by July 1st*
- *Spend one day a month working on strategy, creative endeavors, and business development.*

Sample 90-day strategic plan

Here's a sample 90-day strategic plan to give you an idea of how to pull all of this together.

Vision: *To successfully achieve my sales goal of $35,000 by pulling off an epic Mother's Day Sale, ongoing website sales initiatives, and a wholesale blitz. By the end of the quarter, I'd like to have my marketing process dialed in so that I can hire an assistant to help with social media, ongoing traffic, and email marketing campaigns.*

Theme: *Consistency, Revenue, Goals*

Project #1: *Launch a Mother's Day website campaign*

Goal: *$15,000*

Action steps:

- *Develop a 4-week marketing plan for Mother's Day including the email, text, and social marketing strategy and shipping deadlines by March 15th*
- *Set an ads budget and develop content for the Facebook and Instagram ads by April 1st*
- *Batch content creation for the promotion by April 1st*
- *Create the Mother's Day bundles items for sale by April 10th*
- *Set a date for virtual trunk show event on May 2nd*

Project #2: *Wholesale Outreach campaign*

Goal: *6 new accounts and 6 reorders*

Action steps:

- *Set up an account on Faire by March 5th*
- *Curate new dream store list by March 15th*
- *Send out Wholesale Blitz campaign by outreaching to 10 new stores a week and following up with existing accounts on the 15th of each month*
- *Email line sheets to existing accounts for re-orders*

Project #3: *Develop marketing training manual and hire new Marketing Manager*

Goal: *Completed by June 30th*

Action steps:

- *List out all of the activities I'd like to delegate from marketing*
- *Create a job description and post it to my network and hiring sites by April 30th*
- *Vet, interview, and hire the candidate by May 31st*
- *Set a list of expectations and targets for the new hire*
- *Create and onboarding checklist*
- *Develop two marketing systems a day documenting how I'm doing things with marketing and upload into the SOP folder*
- *Start training the new hire by June 15th*
- *Complete training manual by June 15th*

Growth Planning

A plan for the growth of your business needs to include way more than just where you want your business to go. You need to go holistic on your vision for the future and look at each detail of what you want to achieve with your business. This means looking beyond wanting to make more money or have more time. Without this, your business simply isn't going to grow at the rate you want it to, and you'll likely hit a profit plateau. Without a growth plan, you'll always be flying by the seat of your pants, trying to promote your business but ultimately wasting a lot of time.

Your growth plan needs to connect back to your why and go into each and every business decision you make. It may feel backwards at first, but instead of trying to set goals for your business and hoping you'll have time left over for a personal life, you need to start with how you want to live your life overall and work backwards. This is how you'll create a plan for your business that fits those lifestyle goals.

When I started my first business, my goals mostly had to do with how much money I was making and how much I was selling. It was all in the numbers. I didn't even consider setting a goal for how I wanted to live. I thought if I could sell enough, then I would be happy and successful!

In the beginning, I wanted to be a super-famous designer with my brand and name in stores across the world. I worked my butt off toward those goals until they came true! My collections were sold in over 350 retail stores around the world, incredible places like Sundance Catalog, Anthropologie, Bloomingdales, and ABC Home. Celebrities like Charlize Theron, Halle Berry, and Reese Witherspoon wore my designs. My jewelry was featured in magazines like InStyle, Elle, Real Simple, and the best shopping magazine at the time. It was amazing, but along with all of that success came a schedule I could barely manage. I overworked myself to the point of exhaustion. The worst part was missing out on big family moments because I'd created a business that kept me in my studio or at trade shows all the time. I was totally burned out.

In September 2008, the markets crashed, taking out my wholesale accounts. That's when the bankruptcy notices started coming in—first Red Envelope, then Fortunoff, and then a slew of other small accounts that added up to over $100,000 of uncollected invoices with no inventory to show for it. In October 2007, my company had its best month and shipped $150,000 of wholesale orders. In October 2008, everyone panicked, most of my orders were cancelled or went unpaid, and we shipped a mere $10,000 that month. That's a significant drop, and anyone who knows how cash flow in an inventory business goes knows that this is a terrible pickle to be in.

A few months prior, I hired a consultant, Phil, to help navigate the uncertainty of the times. It was the best decision I ever made. I didn't think I could afford to hire him; it was a scramble to figure out how to pay the $1500/month retainer. Within the first month, I knew I'd made the right choice and quickly discovered I couldn't afford *not* to hire him. During one of our meetings, Phil asked me a question that I couldn't answer right away: *Tracy, what do you love?* As I looked over the mahogany conference table, I thought to myself: *How did I get here?* I was so miserable! I couldn't even form a sentence, and the tears started rolling down my face. My sister (and operations manager) Carlie was sitting across the table from me—looking at me like *suck it up and answer the question.* I finally composed myself long enough to answer and came out with a few things: *I love designing jewelry, I love working with the customers, and I love fine jewelry.* That's when I also got clear on what I didn't want—the stress of the wholesale business in the middle market, aka the business I'd created ... which meant no more selling to stores.

The 2008-9 period was tough for many in the jewelry industry. The rising costs of gold and silver reduced profit margins for brands, retail stores struggled to sell through inventory, and established jewelry companies suffered. I wasn't the only one taken down by the market crash. The events that snowballed after the market crash left me with nearly $400,000 in debt, and I couldn't see a way out of my situation. With help and coaching from Phil and Carlie, we made the tough decision to close down Tracy Matthews Designs, Inc. and I eventually filed for bankruptcy. At the time, I felt like a total failure. It's easy for me to say now, but bankruptcy was a gift in a way because it showed me how to design a business around the lifestyle I wanted for myself and it led me to create the Desired Brand Effect Methodology.

Using the DBE, I designed a new business model that gave me lifestyle freedom and created financial security with low overhead, no full-time employees, and very little inventory on hand. I created a business that allowed me to work remotely instead of having my own studio where jewelers came to. I found jewelers in the NYC diamond district who could produce my products when I had orders. This allowed me to take time off. The business I created started with a clear vision of what success looked like for me: multiple six-figure salary, location independence, travel, and a remote team that didn't require me to be in an office or studio to run my business. When you're thinking about the growth plan for your business, you take into account all of the things that matter most to you..

Take a look at your life and your business. What's working and what's not? Get really clear on what your dream life/business scenario looks like. How are you spending your time? How are you showing up for your family? What does a perfect day in your life look like? How much are you paying yourself? What kind of partnerships and impact are you making in people's lives? How does that feel to you? Now paint a picture of what your life will look like when your business is your dream business. Are you done by 3 pm so that you can pick your kids up at school? Are your mornings free to meditate and exercise? Do you have a team of employees supporting you, or are you doing most of the work yourself? What feels enjoyable?

Here's an example: You only work six hours a day, Monday through Thursday. You interact with your virtual assistant and a few other team members. You mostly spend your time designing new collections and developing business relationships to grow your business. All the day-to-day activities are handled by your team. You go to dance classes most mornings, get home and work for a few hours, have business lunches with influencers and sales reps, and work from a coffee shop most afternoons. You take three vacations a year, one with friends, one with family, and one by yourself. You make $150,000 a year in salary with the majority of your sales coming from online channels. You get paid to speak at local and regional business conferences, and you have a few high-profile custom design clients that help boost your numbers. Plus an email list of 15,000 happy customers!

This is one picture of success, but it doesn't have to be yours. The point is that creating a sustainable growth plan begins with defining what you really desire. Maybe your dream business is having three wholesale accounts while working 12 hours a week and making a part-time income. Maybe you want to have a fully remote business so you can live on a boat and sail around the world.

Your vision for your future growth can be anything you want, but if you make a business plan without considering the lifestyle you want, you'll end up with something you can't sustain. You have to incorporate growth as an absolutely essential aspect of the planning you do, starting right back at the vision stage.

DESIRED BRAND HIGHLIGHT: SS MAGPIE JEWELRY

Cheryl Fuhs from SS Magpie had a vision of leaving her corporate job, living on her sailboat, traveling around the world with her husband, and finding a way to grow her jewelry brand while in retirement. There was only one problem, she needed a way to produce her jewelry in a remote setting.

When she first came to Flourish & Thrive Academy, about 80% of Cheryl's sales were coming from custom projects and consignment partners. This required her to be 'on land' to deliver her products. She needed a new way of doing business, and after taking one of our signature programs, Cheryl clarified her Dream Client and understood how to design cohesive collections. She later revamped her website, created a maker video, and put systems in place to support her future life aboard the boat.

Cheryl was able to automate and delegate several tasks so that she could focus on business growth and being the CVO of her company. Within nine months, Cheryl left corporate America, and is currently living part-time on her sailboat, all while tripling her sales!

Financial Planning

Planning should be strategic at all levels, but especially when it comes to sales. A chapter on strategy wouldn't be complete without stressing how important it is to know your financials. Without clarity around numbers, you can't set SMART goals, because the measurable part is often an income goal when you're running a profitable, sustainable business.

Now, it may feel like sales goals are out of your control, but if you stay consistent you will absolutely start to see results and more predictability in your sales numbers. Not only that, but your business will be more profitable and less stressful if you can read a profit and loss statement, a balance sheet, and a cash flow statement to have a clear understanding of your breakeven point.

Your annual financial plan should determine sales and also include your marketing goals for the year. When your plan is working, you'll know exactly where you're going with your sales, which will lead to consistently exceeding your 'must-have' goals. You'll also be investing and keeping the right amount of profit to reach your personal and business financial goals.

Your quarterly financial goals should align with your annual goals. Keep in mind that for most designers, each quarter looks a little different in terms of realistic sales goals. We know that sales for most jewelry businesses, for example, are highest in the last four months of the year.

Let's say you have a sales goal of $100,000. You might break down the quarterly targets something like this: Q1 $15,000, Q2 $20,000, Q3 $25,000, Q4 $40,000.

Then for each of those quarterly sales goals, make sure the core initiatives you plan on taking on in your 90-day strategic plan are able to meet these numbers. That's the achievable and realistic part of your goal-setting.

Reaching Your Targets and Re-evaluating

Every 90 days, take a step back to evaluate your strategic plan and your progress in relation to your annual goals. If you keep plugging away without tracking your success and evaluating what worked and what didn't, you might be missing out on course-correcting or doubling down on the strategies that work. There's no one-size-fits-all formula for having a successful jewelry company. Remember, success is determined by you, so get clear on what you want—a modest side-hustle, a six-figure lifestyle brand, a multi-million dollar jewelry empire, or something else.

The reason I recommend doing this quarterly and creating a 90-day plan for your next sprint is that nothing will ever get done by only spending your time looking at the big picture. Likewise, if you never stop to evaluate where your efforts are taking you and just say 'yes' to every opportunity, there's a chance you're building a business that's out of alignment with the life you really want. Doing this every quarter gives you enough time to implement and see results, but also is frequent enough if you need to pivot or redirect goals based on the current environment or what you see is working really well. Each time you step back to create a 90-day strategic plan, you're realigning your goals with your vision.

Each 90-day plan begins with reviewing the previous 90 days. Ask yourself these questions:

- What efforts are working?
- What isn't working?
- What did I do well?
- What would I like to do better?
- Did I hit my financial goals for the quarter?
- Where am I in terms of my overall growth plan?

You can use this information to determine which areas need your focus and attention during the next quarter.

There are so many benefits to taking the time to plan out your growth trajectory and financials at the beginning of each year and each quarter. Without your 90-day strategic plan that supports these bigger goals, it will be hard to achieve your vision of success and difficult to execute or focus on the correct actions to meet your goals.

Planning—both wide and narrow—is absolutely essential if you want to create space for your own freedom and creativity, make consistent sales, and avoid being overwhelmed from working on the fly.

CHAPTER 11

SYSTEMS AND AUTOMATION

"Spend time upfront to invest in systems and processes to make long-term growth sustainable."
— JEFF PLATT

At the end of your average workday, does it often feel that you still didn't accomplish everything you set out to do, no matter how hard you worked? When you're swamped with work and overwhelmed with the little stuff, you might be dropping the ball, missing important customer messages, drowning in emails, or constantly putting out fires. You will get pulled in numerous directions on a daily basis until you shift the way you operate.

When you do create that change, it means less stress for you because you're able to prevent the fires from happening in the first place. Many problems in business can be fixed with systems and automation. Most small business owners who are overwhelmed blame their business problems on other people instead of the systems they've created (or lack thereof). As a designer and a visionary, chances are you have resistance to structure. I know I do! However, your visionary side loves results. In order to create results that have the goal of growing and scaling your business, you must start systematizing and automating.

Once I put systems into my own business, my team immediately became more productive and happier. The more we moved towards structure, the more money I saved to reinvest into the business and pay myself—because we cut mistakes in half and employees knew what they were doing. Structure allowed me more time to dedicate to my RGAs and my creative work, because the efficiency of the business was amped up.

Even if you don't have a team (yet), think of all of the things you'd eventually like to get off your plate. The only way you can do that is to document your way of doing things. If you plan to work alone, documented systems can help speed up the time it takes to complete repetitive tasks. And automating parts of your workflow can save you loads of time and increase your impact.

Despite the feelings of resistance you might have around structure, I promise that you will thrive. Yes, I know systems can be daunting or feel hard to create, but just think of it as documenting your way of doing things. This is how you start Scaling Desire—by removing yourself from as much of the hands-on nitty-gritty as possible no matter what stage of business you're in. This chapter is all about creating that structure in a way that works for you.

Why You Need Systems and Automation

Without systems, you may operate in ways that are reactionary to problems. This can end up with you feeling creatively drained and like no one else can do things as well as you can. When you have to be the final decision-maker on everything, you become the biggest bottleneck to your growth. Perhaps you even start becoming a control freak. That's not a good look on you!

If you want to know the fastest way to stop feeling overwhelmed, here's your answer: automate anything you can and systematize your business! This is the ultimate method for creating financial security, lifestyle freedom, and a sense of accomplishment, which is the ultimate goal of the Desired Brand Effect. When you systematize and automate wherever you can, you get more done in less time, which frees you up to work on high-leveraged money making RGAs and the creative parts of the business that you love.

Now, maybe you're thinking: *But I'm a creative and I hate doing admin work and routine tasks!* Well, you're not alone. Most creatives are a mess when it comes to systematizing their businesses. Even if they know they need systems to streamline their results, they make excuses about why they can't do it and avoid creating them. However, if you hate admin work and routine tasks, that's *even more reason* to automate and systematize, because systems focus on those tasks that are most mundane and repetitive so that you don't need to put in the same labor over and over.

Developing better systems allows your business to operate more smoothly on the back end and deliver a better customer experience on the front end. Your Dream Clients will acknowledge this ease by buying more from you. The impact of leaning into this *less enticing* part of your business is profound because it takes some time on the front end but rewards you financially on the back end. Scaling Desire—or removing yourself from the day-to-day of your business—is an exciting phase in your brand journey. This is the part where you get to watch your vision turning into a reality, but it won't happen unless you get the right foundation of systems set up.

What are systems?

Another thing you might be thinking is: *What even is a system? I just do things the way I know how.* And actually, that's perfect, because creating systems doesn't have to be complicated—it's just your way of doing something. Don't overthink it because the hesitation is what causes stress or fear. Let's look at a quick definition to make sure we're on the same page.

Systems are simply a method or way of doing something. For instance, you likely have a specific way that you develop content for social media, make a specific style of jewelry, or engage with your customers or followers through email. All of these items can be documented to speed up the time it takes to complete tasks, prevent problems in your business, and allow you to delegate the things you don't like to do. As a business owner and designer, you have your own unique way of doing things, and this is what we're referring to when we talk about systems. Systems help you streamline your work and get low-level tasks off your plate by taking a major area of your business and making it run more smoothly and efficiently.

In order to grow a profitable business overtime, you have to delegate to elevate. CVOs don't spend their time doing things that a minimum wage earner could do. As they grow, they understand the value in getting low leveraged tasks off their plate so they can hire someone else to do them (even a part time virtual assistant). Systems equip you to hire employees, contractors, and virtual assistants because you'll have a way to train new hires, delegate the jobs that take up your time, and show people your way of doing things. In other words, you work smarter, not harder. When you remove yourself from the day-to-day and delegate—whether that's to a team or even to technology—you can accomplish more in less time. This is the perfect foundation for being able to scale and grow your business.

What is automation?

Automation is just a way to take the 'human' out of the experience to save time and energy on things that can be completed with technology. For instance, you can automate processes with your bookkeeping by connecting your bank accounts to your Quickbooks or Xero account. You can automate certain aspects of your marketing with scheduling tools or email flows that sell for you when someone takes a specific action like buying a piece of jewelry.

Automation in your business will make you more efficient and allow you to sell effortlessly. When you use tools to help create efficiency, you open up space to focus on the high-level tasks that grow your business.

Which Systems to Document

When you begin creating and documenting systems in your business, you might get overwhelmed not knowing where to start or which areas need systems. Here is an overview of the nine most essential areas to systematize. You won't get these all done at once, and that's okay. Focus on documenting a system each time you do something new in your business, and before you know it, you'll have an entire suite of systems recorded that your team can refer to at any time.

Sales

Sales systems include everything you do to bring sales into your business. These will vary depending on your business model but will probably include CRM management, sales scripts and templates, tradeshow and live event systems, customer outreach, and follow-up systems. For ecommerce and online sales, your automated sales funnels are the most crucial of all the systems you'll build so that you can maximize your sales without having to do more 'selling.'

Marketing

Marketing systems include email marketing, social media marketing, public relations and media, direct mail marketing, SEO, advertising, and just about everything you do to promote your business. Remember that marketing is the fuel that feeds the sales engine, and there is crossover. Both are necessary for a thriving business.

Design

Your design systems include many aspects of the design process, including project management, timelines for collection development, sample production, budgets, costing, and pricing, and workflows for one-of-a-kind and custom work.

Production

The production of those designs are an integral part of your systems. Regardless of your business model, you have systems for production and product development. These systems include inventory management, keeping up a production specs bible, production management, ordering supplies, and vendor relationships.

Customer service

Customer service systems are integral to building a business of repeat customers, which everybody wants! These systems include policies, frequently asked questions, protocols on how you respond, follow-up systems, and sales triage. Anything customer-facing is important to include here.

Human resources

When you're ready to hire, having strong policies in place will create structure for your team members to thrive. HR systems cover everything you do to hire or fire people in your business, onboarding, offboarding and training protocols, a process for hiring freelancers, and all the policies they need to follow. Include things like: how to write a job description or your process for hiring the right team and how you interview talent. Include how you review team members, when you review them, and how you develop key performance indicators.

Financial

Financial systems include all the money systems in your business. These might include your bookkeeping process or how you engage with your bookkeeper or accountant, how often you review your finances, what happens in your financial reviews, how profits are distributed, how you track cash flow, and so much more. It might also be directly related to your inventory systems so that you can determine your open to buy and which products you need to sell through. I'd recommend that the first thing you hire are professional service freelancers like a bookkeeper, controller, or accountant. You can track your financials and create robust reporting in accounting programs like Quickbooks or Xero.

Administrative

Administrative systems include basic office management tasks like filing, shipping, ordering supplies, how you package products, and other random tasks. These tasks are some of the first to delegate to an intern or assistant.

Metrics

Tracking and paying attention to the numbers in your business is imperative for growth. You can't measure growth if you aren't tracking it. Metrics to track include social media followers, email and SMS marketing metrics, sales numbers, profit margins, website traffic, conversion rates, bounce rates, and anything you need to measure to be successful. Measure everything possible and gather data that can help you make smart decisions for growth. Quick reminder: set up Google Analytics and use it to make informed decisions.

How to Develop Standard Operating Procedures

Your Standard Operating Procedures (SOPs) are your entire bank of systems that are used to run your company. Your systems are thought of as a bigger function in your business, like how you respond to a return request for a broken piece of jewelry. These include smaller steps (processes) that detail out the actions it takes to reply to the customer and get the piece of jewelry fixed. When you standardize and record your way of doing everything in your business—including best practices, policies, scripts, templates, and processes in each area of your business—you've made a good start at creating your SOPs. By housing these in one place, you're creating what's called an SOP manual.

Any person who comes into your business will be able to read that SOP manual and follow your systems. The great thing about SOPs is that even someone who is coming in to help short-term can quickly learn the way things are done in your business without much training. Whether you want to go away on vacation or hire a full-time employee, you can delegate tasks quickly and know they'll be done the right way.

You may think activities you do on a daily basis are self-explanatory, but when you start outsourcing and hiring more employees, training will be a *nightmare* if you don't have your systems clearly documented. The biggest complaint I hear from brands when they attempt to hire without a proper SOP manual in place is this: *it's easier to do it myself.* So they end up giving up on delegating, which keeps them in a loop of feeling over-whelmed because they don't have enough support. In order to avoid confusion, mistakes, and losses, you have to document your way of doing things or you will set yourself up for failure anytime you try to get things off your plate. Keep in mind that a lot of the tasks you do are second nature to you, but other people might have a different way of doing things or not have the same level or attention to detail. Perhaps their level of under-standing and sophistication is actually better than yours. Either way, you should document *your way* of doing things and continually update and optimize the system and processes for better results.

The good news is you probably already know your entire operations by heart. Now you just need to find a way to document it quickly. The easiest way to create an operations manual is to record what you normally do each time you perform a task or change the way you do something. I'll share some quick ways to document that don't require hours of writing momentarily. First, let's walk through the steps of documenting your first systems and starting to build your SOP manual:

Step 1: Identify the task

Start with the systems you know will always be around. For many jewelry brands, this includes: manufacturing, production, shipping, customer service, and training. Prioritize the lowest leveraged tasks that are repetitive, anything you'd like to get off your plate, or tasks you consistently do to keep your business functioning.

Step 2: Purpose for the system

Why do you even need this system? Make sure all of your tasks are worth the time and effort and that the system has a purpose. If you can't come up with a purpose for your system, you don't need it.

Step 3: Break it down

Typically, an SOP manual will include systems, processes and workflows, and a breakdown of policies, best practices, templates, scripts, and training.

A policy is a set of guidelines or rules you use in your business, whereas a best practice is your most effective way of doing something. A template is a starting point, script or file that is pre-formatted so it can be used in different scenarios over and over again.

Step 4: Record the way you do it

Now record how you do the things you do. You don't need to get into too much detail at first. Your SOP manual is a working document that you continue to update as you evolve, so keep it simple. Jot down or record your screen with the basic steps of what you do or how each task should be completed.

While simplicity is best, make sure to include anything you feel is important for you and your team to understand when completing the task.

Here are some tools that can help you create a record of your systems quickly:

- ◆ Camera and/or smartphone
- ◆ Screen recording tools like Loom, Screencastify or Screenflow
- ◆ Transcription tools like Otter.ai, Scribie or Rev.com
- ◆ A cloud-based organization platform like Process Street, Google Drive or Dropbox
- ◆ Project management tool like Asana or Trello
- ◆ Password protection software like LastPass
- ◆ Other apps or tools to store your systems (optional)

Check out more resources at DesiredBrandEffect.com/resources.

Step 5: Checklists

Systems and processes should be backed by checklists, as these help ensure no step is missed along the way. The checklist acts as a shortlist of all the steps that need to happen in order for the system to be done correctly. I like checklists because they ensure the nitty-gritty gets completed even when tasks get delegated. Make a checklist of steps as a cheat sheet for the system.

Step 6: Extras

Reread everything you wrote down and ask yourself: If I put someone else in charge of this task, would they need more information? Aim for simple, but make sure you answer all possible questions so anyone using the system doesn't need to ask.

Step 7: Test it out

Give the system document to one of your team members or someone who has never completed this task before. See if they can complete the task using your guide without having to ask any extra questions. Then ask them if there's anything else they think you should add.

Step 8: Communicate

Now it's time to put your system to work! Give it out to everyone on your team who is involved in the task. Make sure the system is in the format best suited for them to learn. Instructions can include text, checklists, visuals, or a quick video. Even if you don't have a team yet, you might at some point when you need help. In the meantime, use the guidelines you created to provide consistency in your own work and keep a copy in a safe place for the future.

Step 9: Complete your operations manual

If you repeat the steps above each time you create a system, pretty soon you'll have all of the material you need for an operations manual. Compile it all into a cloud-based document like Google Drive or keep your systems in your project management tool for safe keeping. Using cloud storage is important so you don't lose your work, you have a place where multiple people can access the latest copy, revisions are made in real time, and you don't put yourself at risk for hard-drive failure and the loss of your SOP manual.

The most important part of your SOP manual is to create something you can use to speed up efficiency, get support when needed, and keep your operations flowing easily. Keep updating your manual as your business evolves.

Automation

Even with standard operating procedures, there is potential for problems to creep in when other humans take on tasks. Human error is always possible! However, if you can automate your systems using technology, there is huge potential for your business to flow even more smoothly.

Getting more done with less time is one of the biggest goals and results of Scaling Desire. With the right automations, you can spend fewer hours in your business, get more done, and make more money. Technology and tools not only reduce the chance of human error, but they speed up results in your business with less effort. With a little up-front work of getting some automations set up, you can reap some great ongoing rewards.

Types of automation

Technology gives you an easy way to create systems anyone can follow or that need no input at all. You can use tech to automate workflows, systems and processes in your business, as well as marketing and sales funnels. If you put the right systems in place from the start, you won't need to reinvent the wheel with every project, client, or new hire, but where should you start?

Some of the main places to begin automating with tried-and-true tech and tools are: marketing (especially email marketing), CRMs and databases, inventory management systems, project management systems, time management systems and scheduling tools, productivity tools, bookkeeping software, and communication tools.

Marketing automations

Even though it will be important to create systems in all the areas of your business that I mentioned above, there's one area where automating will carry a lot of weight and has great potential for making you more money and helping you get seen—marketing. When you've tested your concept and you know what sells, automating the processes that help more people find you can make a huge impact on your growth.

I explained earlier how powerful an automated sales funnel can be to increase your sales, and now it's time to create specific email sequences that steer the prospect toward a purchase and follow up on auto-pilot. Not all emails can be automated. Some will be broadcast, which means written and sent out on a certain date such as newsletters, content emails, or time-sensitive promotional emails. Email automations are a bit different.

These are email sequences that are set up in advance to go out automatically once someone takes an action. The sequence of emails is triggered automatically when someone opts in to a lead magnet or takes a specific action, adding items to a shopping cart without checking out or buying something from you.

There are some highly effective email sequences that I recommend you include in your marketing automations. The five core ones that I suggest setting up so that you can make sales while you sleep are:

A nurture sequence that goes out automatically when someone opts-in to your email list. It delivers value and moves people toward a sale.

A post-purchase sequence that goes out to confirm the order, ask for a review or feedback, and move people towards sharing or purchasing again.

An abandoned cart sequence to recapture people who didn't complete their purchase.

A win-back campaign to engage people who previously purchased but have not reordered in a long time.

A sunset sequence or list cleanse campaign to remove people from your email list after a period of being inactive.

There are other kinds of email sequence that you can add when you need, so once you have your five core automations working for you, begin thinking about other things to automate. Perhaps you can create automation to follow up with wholesale accounts, live event attendees, e-commerce buyers who buy a specific product, or visitors on your website. For the sake of this book, these five core automations are the ones you should implement first. I don't want to overwhelm you with too many options, but as you feel more confident, you can become more sophisticated and complex in your marketing automations.

Email automation should be hooked up to any place that someone can opt-in to your email list throughout your website and any connected landing pages. Make sure that you exclude anyone in an automated campaign from regular email broadcasts for the period that they're inside the campaign. Once your automated campaign is over, you can include this segment of your email list into other email broadcasts and special promotions.

Speaking of complexity, it's important to choose and email CRM or software that lets you set up sequences that can drive better results and keep leads active. Email CRM software can be complex, so you also need to make sure you're actually going to learn how to use it! Automation lets you interact with more clients in more ways in more places, but it requires more tech savviness than a simple one-off broadcast email. That said, you can set it up once and reap rewards over and over, so it's well worth automating this area of your business as a priority because it has so much potential for growth.

The other great thing about automated email sequences is that you can create email flows based on client behavior. When you notice trends in data, you can segment your email list based on when people last purchased, when they last opened an email, or even how people are interacting with your email content.

If you're worried about emailing too much and annoying your customers or subscribers, remember these people signed up for your list and want to hear from you. When you email consistently, you show your audience you're reliable by nurturing your relationship with them.

Remember, if you're feeling intimidated by setting this up, you have options. You can learn how to do this yourself in programs like our Laying the Foundation and Momentum programs. You can also hire email automation experts to do the work for you once you have your emails written. Try to view this as an opportunity rather than a burden, and start where you are, even if that's with your very first welcome sequence.

According to media platform Disruptive Advertising, 72% of people say they would rather receive promotional content through email than social media. Therefore, automating your emails is one of the greatest resources a growing brand can invest time and effort in. E-commerce is changing the way things are bought and sold, and it's near impossible to stay at the top of your game without a solid marketing automation strategy, so I encourage you to set these up now!

Semi-automations with CRMs

Another area where you can semi-automate relationship-building is with a good sales CRM. Depending on your business model, some of this can be done using tools like Klaviyo or Omnisend. If you have a more high-touch business where there is a lot of personal interaction with your clients, you might consider a more robust sales CRM that's used for the purpose of relationship building and follow up. This is one of the best investments any designer can make in their business, because a good CRM can manage, organize, and analyze all of your customer interactions throughout the course of your relationship with a prospective account or current customer. No matter how good your memory is, as your brand grows, you simply can't remember every detail about every client! A CRM helps you do that.

Your CRM will not only keep customer information organized, but also helps you remember who you're supposed to follow up with and when. You can use your CRM for follow up on reorders, client anniversaries and birthdays, complimentary ring maintenance, and just about anything you need. Sales are the lifeblood of your business, and your repeat customers are your ticket to increasing sales!

There are lots of options for CRMs, including HubSpot, Insightly, Pipedrive, Zendesk (formerly Base), Contactually, or Zoho. This type of CRM is slightly different to the CRM you'd use for robust marketing automations because these platforms are designed for robust individual customer interactions like wholesale outreach or custom clients. Ideally, the CRM system that you choose will track your orders as well as your customers. Then any time you're speaking with a client, you have detailed information of what they've purchased right in front of you.

A robust CRM will also show you the information you need about customers, remind you when to follow up, and keep you focused on the customer relationships. They're especially useful when you're doing one-of-a-kind or custom work, individual client outreach, and wholesale. Play around with your options, because a marketing automation CRM like Klaviyo or Omnisend might have enough features if you aren't actively selling to individuals or stores.

DESIRED BRAND HIGHLIGHT: ACID QUEEN JEWELRY

One of our superstar students, Alex Camacho of Acid Queen Jewelry, completely adopted the many facets of the Desired Brand Effect in her business after joining our Momentum program. She had a simple goal of growing her business to $100,000 a year in annual revenue and she was seeking out mentorship and support to get outside eyes on her business.

By building her audience, adapting her marketing

as algorithms changed, setting goals that supported her vision for success, and then backing that up with the systems and automation to help her grow, Alex's business grew incredibly fast. Essentially, she laid the groundwork of a sales funnel so that when she started running ads, she was able to scale her sales.

Within 18 months, Alex grew from $65,000 to $150,000 in annual revenue. One year later, she more than doubled that number and ended 2020 with $330,000 during the global pandemic. Alex would be the first to tell you it's not as much about the "money," it's about building a community and what that financial security offers her.

With structure and systems in place in her business, Alex was able to take a month off to travel Thailand with her husband, buy a home, hire an employee, and hike for two hours every day. She built a business that supports her vision of success.

Creatives Need Space to be Creative!

Creating systems for your business goes beyond what you, your employees, or your contractors do on a daily basis. Modern business owners are lucky enough to have access to incredible technology for automation, which can lighten the load and make repetitive tasks happen effortlessly. The great thing about automations and tech systems is that they run themselves after a little up-front effort, and they will save you tons of time and even increase your sales. In short, they speed up results.

When you get this piece down, you're going to feel the relief that comes with having control over your destiny, in the same way as when using those time-saving tools we covered earlier. Even those productivity platforms are automations in themselves. See how they're everywhere!

I've stepped you through the how-to of systems, but I want to urge you not to reinvent the wheel here. There are plenty of tools, tech, and templates already out there that can make your life easier. We include a lot of done-for-you scripts and templates in our Flourish & Thrive Academy programs that are specific to jewelry and handmade business owners. While I encourage you to make them yours and shape them to work for your specific business, know that you don't have to start from scratch.

If you've been feeling overwhelmed and stressed out in your business for a while now, I highly recommend setting aside some time to create systems and automation in your business. Without these tools, you might eventually burn out or lose out on growing your sales because you can't manage any more in the time you have.

When you get stuck in the grind of the day-to-day of your business, not only will you fail to scale, you might also end up miserable, wondering how the business you started out of passion has grown to be such a time and energy suck. Creating systems and automations is the fastest way to scale your sales and profits and remove yourself from things that drain your creativity and slow your growth.

If you're ready to stop being reactive in your business and step up your systems, commit to giving some of these a try.

CHAPTER 12

GETTING THE
RIGHT SUPPORT

"The best executive is the one who has sense enough to pick good men to do what he wants done, and self-restraint enough to keep from meddling with them while they do it."

— THEODORE ROOSEVELT

If you want to scale your business to the next level, you need to surround yourself with support from people who have been where you want to go. Support comes in many forms, including being part of a like-minded community, working with a consultant, coach or mentor, hiring employees or contractors, and outsourcing production or finding a manufacturer.

Finding a supportive community of like-minded individuals is a complete game-changer for solo-business owners because it gives people who can't hire big teams or individual consulting a place to get feedback. We know that one of the most powerful ways to grow a company is through collaboration (over competition) because this is how the best ideas rise to the top. Without this important tool in business, many creative founders feel isolated and lonely, which causes them to burn out and make mistakes that could be prevented. Community can also create that emotional lift, inspire you to be better, and be a space to root others on. You'll accomplish more with a like-minded community around you than you ever would on your own.

At a certain point, you'll also want to get outside eyes on your business. That might look like taking a program for continuing education, or working with a consultant or coach to show you what you can't see because you're too close to it. Today, I run three profitable businesses and I attribute much of my success to the coaches and consultants that I've hired.

Support doesn't stop there, of course, because you have support from within your business in the form of a team. Hiring a team doesn't have to mean a bunch of employees coming into your office every day. It might look like that, but these days the gig economy allows you to build a small and mighty team of part-time freelancers, interns, and virtual assistants (from around the world) without having to employ people from the get-go.

One thing is certain—when you scale, you won't be able to do everything by yourself. If you try, you'll hit roadblocks, so finding these layers of support as you grow is the best way to stay strong, grounded, and stress-free. Remember, most jewelry makers start a business because they have a passion for making or selling jewelry. Instead of being a business owner, they create a job for themselves and operate from an employee mentality. If this sounds like you, this chapter will help you shift your role so that whatever you dream of becomes a reality.

Finding a Community of Like-Minded Peers

One of the benefits of being an entrepreneur or solopreneur is the freedom and flexibility it offers, but this benefit is also the biggest downfall. No matter what anyone tells you, business ownership can be a lonely and isolating career choice. Some days you might feel like you're the only one going through what you're going through, and it can be paralyzing not having anyone to bounce ideas off of, even if you are normally an independent and decisive person.

Having a group of like-minded people you can share ideas with, get feedback from, and give advice to gives you the essential collaboration needed in business. It's a place where you can solve problems that you've never encountered before and challenge you to become a better business owner. This kind of network keeps you emotionally supported and encouraged through the wild ride of entrepreneurship.

When I started my first business, I didn't have this at all, despite trying to create it with some close friends who were in the industry. In fact, I tell the story of me asking a dear friend where she got her hangtags (the little silver tag that hangs on the back of a necklace) and she told me: *I can't give you my resources because that takes away my competitive edge.* That moment has been emblazoned in my mind for 20 years because it wasn't a big ask. This experience is one of the reasons Flourish & Thrive Academy came into being—I wanted to create a community of like-minded jewelry makers who were open to sharing because they realized that a rising tide lifts all boats.

Others have worried that competition and copying is inevitable in a like-minded community. That mindset is detrimental because when you have the right attitude, you come from a place of service and realize that you get what you give. In the past, I have seen a lot of competition amongst designers, worrying that someone was going to steal their ideas and cause them to lose their competitive edge. This is why our main focus at Flourish & Thrive Academy has been curating an amazing community of ambitious designers who *collaborate* with one another while receiving high-level coaching to build their brands. In testimonials from our community, you'll frequently hear designers say that they learn just as much from their fellow designers as they do from the coaches. Our motto? "Community and collaboration over competition." The members of our community help each other out and are in support of one another's growth. It can even lead to collaborations between brands. That's the kind of community you want to find!

To find the right support in a like-minded community, you might want to try joining masterminds, networking groups, courses with a coaching component, or coaching programs. All of these have their own benefits. When I joined my first mastermind, my business grew so quickly because I learned new ideas that I hadn't thought of, got out of my regular thinking process, and became inspired to do something different. Without that group, I wouldn't have had the idea to start Flourish & Thrive Academy. As an added bonus, I've created friendships with other designers that have helped all of our businesses grow.

When you find a community you love and start participating in groups, show up with the spirit of helpfulness and encouragement. If fear-based thoughts sneak in telling you someone might steal your ideas or you'll lose your competitive edge, try to let those go. While it's possible someone might want to steal your idea, if you're clear about your brand, your value, and your Dream Client Avatar, the competition won't matter. Remember, when you're selling specifically to *your* unique Dream Clients, even though there will always be other people doing something similar, they're never going to be *you*. The benefits you'll gain by being part of a community of like-minded individuals will far outweigh the potential of someone taking advantage.

DESIRED BRAND HIGHLIGHT:
CHARLIE MADISON ORIGINALS

Wendy Hively started a jewelry brand to support
a cause she is passionate about: helping programs

that support military families. She had made decent progress on her own. However, with a full-time government job, she had little time to grow her jewelry business, so she knew she needed mentorship to help uncover her blind spots if she was going to progress any further.

With our 90-day strategic planning and the support of our mentoring program, Wendy has been meeting or *exceeding* her sales goals every single quarter. Her profit margins grew by 30% and the accountability helped her stay on track to hit her goal to have a six-figure side hustle. And she did it. She attributes much of her recent success to the support she received from our coaches and a community of like-minded jewelry designers.

Wendy's commitment to her success is palpable. If she can grow her company to six figures with lower price-point jewelry while working a full-time job, so can anyone. I can only imagine what Wendy would be capable of if Charlie Madison Originals was a full-time business.

Getting Outside Eyes on Your Business

Working with a coach or mentor in a one-on-one or group coaching program is powerful. It helps you move a lot faster toward your goals. They can help personalize advice, help you become more efficient, and get you unstuck. There's a lot you can learn from programs and self-education, but there's nothing like having the advice and accountability of someone who truly understands the business you're in and has done what you're trying to achieve for themselves or others. You may have heard the saying *the fastest path to growth is learning from others who've already done what you're trying to achieve.* That's because they've already gone where you want to go, so it's easy for them to help prevent you from getting blindsided by issues and overcome potential roadblocks.

The most important takeaway here is that the right coach or mentor can see problems that you can't see yourself. They can also see where you are progressing when you have a hard time seeing that for yourself. When you're working in your business every day, it's hard to see what's in front of you objectively. With the right coaching and mentorship, you can focus on your role as CVO rather than staying stuck in a growth plateau.

I believe in this so strongly that I am almost always working with an executive coach, mentor, or consultant to help me with whatever I am trying to achieve. For instance, I joined a mastermind group that helped me leap from a low-six-figure business to a seven-plus-figure business within three years in a niche market. Earlier I shared my story of my consultant, Phil, who opened my eyes to more than I ever expected. I've been in coaching programs to help with sales, leadership, and marketing and also regularly work with consultants to help my team run more efficiently. When I look back at the results in my own company, I can track the times of serious growth back to working with a coach or consultant. That growth happened not just due to the knowledge I acquired but the accountability to implement and what I said I would. If you notice that you aren't following through or moving quickly enough, you might need more accountability!

I'm a huge advocate of working with coaches and mentors at all levels of business, especially when you need specific advice or you're tackling something new-to-you. If you aren't in a place to make the investment in a coach, mentor, or consultant, accountability can come from your community, too. Even if you're super motivated, sometimes it's hard to take action on the things that are most going to grow your business. A business mentor, an accountability partner, or a mastermind group is essential to staying on track and in alignment with your vision. Working with a coach allows you to get the focused, one-on-one attention your business needs. Instead of figuring things out on your own, you'll have built-in feedback and guidance to help you succeed. The result of this kind of support is almost always increased profitability.

My team of coaches and I would be honored to support you in your business growth. In our coaching program, for example, our designers have access to experts in a multitude of areas, including sales, website optimization, wholesale, SEO, email marketing, content development, and customer relationships. This is a huge bonus to joining a mastermind since buyers, designers, and other industry experts don't usually share trade secrets openly with emerging designers. These are the kinds of access and connections you can only get through a program where you have seasoned professionals dedicated to supporting you in your success.

For more information on getting support for your business, head on over to FlourishThriveAcademy.com/strategy and apply for a free strategy audit.

Hiring Contractors and Employees

One of the biggest transitions you'll face as a business owner is letting go of the need to do everything yourself. All great business owners have one thing in common: they know that in order to reach their goals and grow a business, they'll eventually need to hire out or delegate their weaknesses. That starts with hiring others—freelancers, contractors, and employees—to take things off their plate. When you have the *right* team, you'll be able to step into your role as Chief Visionary Officer, because the low-leveraged tasks will be taken care of and your focus will be on executing the bigger vision of your brand.

I hate to break it to you, but you aren't good at everything, and the amount of time you waste trying to improve your weaknesses is actually pulling your business down. That's exactly why in Scaling Desire, we talk about documenting systems and automating things in your business—so that you can delegate the things you don't like, aren't good at, or aren't the best use of your time.

The first step to delegating is to acknowledge that you don't have to do everything yourself. It's okay to ask for help, and if you need a sign you aren't making progress, here it is. The next step is to understand when to delegate. It's fairly simple—you don't have enough time in the day to get the most important things done. You often feel overwhelmed or chaotic with your workflow. What you used to do is no longer working anymore, or your business is backsliding into a sales plateau or decline. Something has got to change if you're in this place. If you want to keep growing, it might be time to take things off your plate so you can free up your headspace and be more strategic with your time.

As we covered in Chapter 11, delegating begins with systems and automations. Not everything can be done with technology or a system, and that's when it's time to find the right people to bring on to your team. Before we take a look at when to hire people for your business, I want to ask you a question: *What happens when life happens? Does your business stop if you stop working?* It's a question that a lot of business owners don't consider because they probably don't think about it often.

DESIRED BRAND HIGHLIGHT:
TWYLA DILL DESIGNS

When I first met Twyla Dill, she'd just had her best year in business. With this sense of accomplishment, she also had some difficult choices to make. Twyla knew that her mother's death was imminent, as she was terminally ill. That's when Twyla asked for our support to help set up systems in her business so that she could hire help and take time off to grieve.

During the previous year, her already-successful business brought in nearly $150,000 and she had a goal to meet or exceed that number the following year. She didn't want her sales to backslide due to this tragic life event.

Within three months of implementing the Desired Brand Effect in her business, she was able to hire her first employee, as well as a production assistant. Her online sales in the first quarter increased by 72% over the same period the previous year. During the three months she took off, Twyla made more money than she had in the same timeframe the previous year. July was usually a slow month for her, but she closed $30,000 in sales, making it her best month in the history of her business. By the end of the year, she had increased her total sales by 33% to $200,000.

When the pandemic hit and Twyla was forced to stop doing in-person shows, she leaned further into email automation and digital marketing to replace her lost income. The systems she had in place allowed her to thrive during a difficult time. When things opened up again, Twyla had the hiring SOPs and systems to rehire a team. At the time this book was written, Twyla was on track to end the year with $300,000 in annual sales, a big increase over her previous best year.

Her results were so incredible for two reasons. First, her business didn't stop when she needed to take time off. And second, she was able to be nimble when times changed. Twyla can do much more in less time and her business doesn't rely on her to grow.

I featured Twyla on the Thrive by Design podcast and you can listen to the episode at FlourishThriveAcademy.com/Twyla.

When to hire

After hearing Twyla's story, you might be wondering when to hire and who to hire first. For every brand, this is a personal decision. Typically the clear indicator is that you can't grow any further without additional help, or you know that if you bring someone on it will help you grow a lot more quickly. It might feel scary to hire your first employee or contractor because it is a big leap of faith and a financial commitment. You might not even know what to delegate or have concerns that they might not do as good of a job as you. Those fears are normal.

So, where do you start adding the right people? The general rule of thumb is to bring people on slowly to take over low leveraged tasks. I'd recommend bringing someone on sooner than you think, as long as you're motivated to train them and focus on the revenue needed to support their compensation. You'll quickly see how much more productive you are when you can pass off some of the daily tasks to a VA or contractor and focus your attention on your RGAs. Even if you're not ready to hire a full team, you can—and I say *must*—start hiring out basic, low-level tasks to a virtual assistant ASAP. Hiring a virtual assistant to do small but time-consuming tasks like shipping orders and managing social media posts gives you time to focus on strategy.

Thinking back to the 75% rule, here are some questions you can ask to know if you're ready to hire the next person for your team.

- Will I be able to focus on higher leveraged revenue-generating activities or activities that only I can do?
- Will the business bring in more profit if I hire an assistant, contractor, or employee?
- Am I currently able to spend the majority of my time on the actions that are bringing money into the business?
- Am I ending each day with tons of unfinished repetitive tasks on my plate?

If you answered yes to any of those questions, it's time to start hiring your team. Even if you don't think you're completely ready, develop your systems, create a budget for hiring, focus on your RGAs, and take a leap of faith. You'll enjoy getting things off your plate and being less overwhelmed.

Who to hire

In general, it's best to hire a freelancer or virtual assistant as a contractor with a specific skill set as opposed to employees when you're first starting out. The gig economy has allowed so much more flexibility for people to work from home, which is great for the freelancer and less of a long-term financial responsibility for you. Depending on the role, they can usually work remotely, use their own tools or computer, and set their own hours, which allows you to hire from a variety of locations instead of just your local area. Eventually, you can hire office staff and interns for part-time or full-time employment.

When you step into your role as CVO and leader of your company and team, you'll be far more effective with the right team around you. Whatever type of support you hire, you've got to make sure you're bringing on the right people and that requires proper vetting. The traditional way of hiring by just looking at a resume then having a few short interviews with someone doesn't necessarily help you find the best candidate. Some people are really great interviewers while others might be nervous during the interview and appear not to perform as well. It starts with understanding exactly what you're looking for and hiring for skill set instead of personality.

Once, I posted an ad for an entry-level assistant and got 90 applications in the first few days. The high response came from the fact that the ad talked about what kind of company the job was for and named qualities I was looking for in a candidate. The position was specifically for someone who was a superstar but just starting out in their career. The ad said things like, "Are you excited to be in a support role for a quickly growing online business?" and "Are you a highly organized person who thrives on seeing projects through to completion?" This language gave applicants the opportunity to self-select and decide whether they felt like a good fit for the company. The ad also listed who the job was *not* for, which helped weed out career VAs who were not a good fit.

When I hired my executive assistant, I vetted her through a hiring funnel that I created. I narrowed down the applicants to the top three who made it through the verbal interview. Then I took them through the final step of the hiring hurdle, a paid test project. I had both candidates do the exact same job so I could see how they performed, and some interesting information comes out of that. My second candidate bowed out of the hiring competition, my top candidate did a terrible job with the work (although she was a great interviewer), and my last candidate did an amazing job, which was surprising. She had no industry experience, unlike the others, but I paid attention to the quality of work she did. That executive assistant worked for me part-time for four years until she graduated from acupuncture school. She'll be hard to replace.

When you're hiring, rather than posting a job description that simply states what kinds of tasks they'll be doing, consider what kind of person you want on the team. The hiring process requires you to focus on what kind of vibe and culture you want in your company, not just what activities need to be completed. Once you have written your ad, post in a variety of places including your website, social media platforms, Craigslist, college job boards, and job listing sites.

Interviewing and selecting candidates is something you'll get a feel for over time. Be wary of hiring someone just because you like them. Instead, focus on skill set, experience, personality, communication, and preparedness. You can take notes during an interview and rank those areas on a scale of 1–5. Another way to examine your prospects is to cross-reference the qualities they have with the skills you need for the position. For example, a candidate for data entry or wire wrapping doesn't have to be the bubbly type, but they need to be accurate. If they're social, they'll probably be less efficient. In that case, you would look for qualities like detail-oriented, time management skills, and good with their hands. On the other hand, a social and bubbly prospect for sales, PR, or marketing would be a great fit!

Once you bring on your first hires, don't forget to include a trial period for 30, 60, or 90 days. I've hired many people in my time, and nearly every time I've skipped this step, the person didn't work out. They interviewed well and had all of the right answers, but when it came to actually doing the work, they were not a good fit. You can test their work by giving them a paid test project, asking for samples of their work, or both. Once you select the candidate, make sure you set check-in points and you properly "onboard" and "train" candidates. These check-in points should be at the 30-, 60-, and 90-day periods. If they are a great fit into the skill set you need and a culture fit for the company, you've hired a winner.

As you build a team around you, focus on the leadership skills you want to embody, and remember it's part of your role to manage your people and keep them on track until you have someone who can do that for you. You'll want to track things like tasks, goals, and milestones in their work. Ideally, you'd have a scorecard system where you track key performance indicators or KPIs. This could happen through project management platforms, a Google spreadsheet, a daily check-in call or message, or a weekly team meeting. It's your role as the leader and CVO of your brand to inspire, support, and manage your people while maintaining strong boundaries and giving them space to do their own work. It comes down to striking a balance between being hands-on and giving people space to make mistakes, think for themselves, and learn and grow in their role.

Lastly, make sure you're documenting your hiring processes, onboarding protocols, weekly scorecard system, and daily to-dos in your SOP manual, which we covered in the last chapter.

Leadership

You can't grow a business trying to do everything yourself. This is probably the most important element you need to embrace in order to step into your role as CVO. Legit business owners and entrepreneurs don't spend their time doing things they could hire an intern to do, so start acting the part! If you don't already, it's time to start identifying as a leader. By starting a business and following your passion, you're choosing to lead your own life, so leading a team through your vision and brand impact is the next step.

The way you show up as a leader plays out both in your overall brand vision, as well as the way you manage your team. Think about a few people you admire, whether they're personal connections or public figures, and what leadership qualities they have. Then consider which of those qualities you want to embody as you grow your brand and your team. Lead by example by regularly sharing your company vision, praising and empowering team members for doing a good job, and taking corrective actions when team members aren't doing their job. When you hire support around you, keep in mind the areas you enjoy leading and managing and which areas you would rather pass on to someone else. And when you communicate with and train your team, remember those leadership qualities that matter to you!

When it's not working out

You might have heard the term: *be slow to hire and quick to fire.* That holds true, because sometimes it just doesn't work out. There's no two ways around it—firing people sucks. But you'll be doing yourself and the team member a favor since if someone isn't performing in their job, they're likely unhappy anyway. This is precisely why it's important to have regular check-ins with your team members and have some sort of scorecard system that you can rate their performance with. Typically, you want to give three corrective actions and share clear expectations so that they can try to improve over time. If at that point it's not a fit, let them go.

Make sure you document in your files what's happening, the corrective actions you're taking, and record or screenshot any interactions or relevant data. You'd keep this on record in your HR file in case someone tries to retaliate later. This is rare for a small business, but it does happen. In 2008, I hired a PR intern who wasn't working out. During her training period, she was hired as an independent contractor and we'd planned to bring her on as an employee after the trial period. We let her go within a 45-day period and she tried to take legal action. It was a good reminder to document everything.

There are times when you might also have to lay off a team member due to shifts in the market or a lack of work. Once again, this sucks, but remember the financial health of your company is more important than feeling obligated to keep someone employed when you can't afford to.

In either case—hiring or laying off a team member—make sure that you have an offboarding process and conduct an exit interview. If someone tries to take legal action later, your well-documented files and strict onboarding and offboarding protocols will be a game changer.

Surrounding yourself with the right support—a team, a community, and a coach and/or consultant—is where you have true potential for moving out of that Maker Mindset we talked about in Chapter 1 and instead showing up for your business as the brand's Chief Visionary Officer. If you want a business that can grow, scale, and give you freedom, this is your wake-up call to step into the role of CVO and lead with support. In the next and final chapter, we're going to focus on achieving that mindset and help you fully embody being a leader in your business.

PART FOUR:

TYING IT ALL TOGETHER

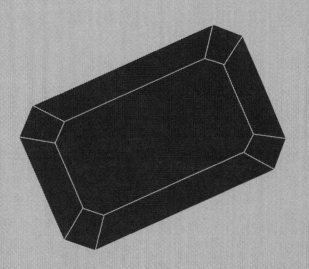

CHAPTER 13

MAKING THE DESIRED BRAND EFFECT WORK FOR YOU

"The story of the starving artist is a myth."
— JEFF GOINS

You're a maker, a creator, an expert in your craft, but do you know what else you are for your brand and business? You're a visionary leader, and visionary leaders bring direction, determination, stability and balance to their business, with the mindset of leading from the front.

If you've come this far in the book, you likely have a lot of ideas swirling around in your brain. I can totally relate! If that's the case, then I'd like you to take a pause here. It's such an asset to have a mind that works in this way. You'll never be short of ideas, that's for sure. However, trying to implement all the things at once to make giant leaps in your business can be just as detrimental as not doing anything. Why? Because starting fifteen things and not finishing any of them will never get you the results that you could get from starting three things, doing them really well, and following right through to the end.

So, how do you know where you are on the Desired Brand Effect model and what to tackle first?

Have You Hit a Gap?

As I mentioned in Chapter 2, each pillar of the Desired Brand Effect will help you to grow your business in some way. When you're in a growth zone, you're likely to see consistent sales success, because you're attracting attention and building an aligned audience that wants, loves and desires your jewelry; loyalty from those buyers, because of your exceptional service and relationships that you've built; and more ease in your business, because your business is scaling in profits and impact.

There is a lot of crossover because success in one area has a trickle effect in other areas of your business. On the flipside, it can force you to level up in areas that aren't doing so well. This is what I call the 'gaps' of the Desired Brand Effect, and they're actually super helpful, even though they might be frustrating you right now, because they signal where you need change in your business.

If we're looking at the Desired Brand Effect Model, the first gap typically happens when people are in the startup phase. That gap is represented by slow or inconsistent sales, which means you need to focus on

Creating Desire and Sharing Desire for your brand. Take a look at your audience. Are they resonating with your products? Are you putting yourself out there and marketing enough? Are you doing the right RGAs on a regular basis? Does your brand voice create a connection with your Dream Clients? Is your collection fully developed and merchandised? Investigate the reasons why you're in the rollercoaster sales cycle and focus on consistent sales practices.

The next gap is a profit or growth plateau. This gap is characterized by a period of stagnation, working very hard or harder than before but not seeing your sales grow. You've gotten to a glass ceiling that you can't break through. This typically happens in the gap between Sharing Desire and Scaling Desire. You might consider looking at where you're spending your time and how efficient you're being. At this point, it's time to start getting things off your plate so that you can focus on the higher-leveraged money-making RGAs and delegate the busy work. Have you started creating SOPs so that you can hire a virtual assistant or a team member? Are you delivering a great customer experience and automating marketing to help improve retention and repeat sales? Are you finding ways to get coaching or support so that you aren't working in a silo? Investigate how you can streamline and optimize what you're already doing well and start delegating tasks that don't need to be done by you.

The worst gap is a business backslide or a brand disconnect, which happens when Scaling Desire and Creating Desire are out of alignment. This typically happens when you're trying to be everything to everyone or you've lost focus of what's important by getting caught up in trends or targeting the wrong audience. It might be that you need to revisit your systems, what's being automated, and how those things tie into your goals. It might also be a sign of the wrong people on your team, poor leadership, or that you need to take a step back and re-evaluate your brand in general. This is the hardest to overcome if you aren't honest and objective. Get some objective eyes on your business to help you figure out what you're missing.

You need all three pillars of the Desired Brand Effect to launch, grow and scale a successful business. I like to think of these pillars as levels in school because the work is never done. You can always grow your audience, expand your sales, and create operational efficiencies that help increase your profitability and impact. What you put into the model is what you get out of it.

If you don't know where you are or you haven't been able to see any sales trends yet in your business, start at the beginning with the Creating Desire pillar and go from there. Having that clarity about your business will help you as you cycle through the pillars.

Reminder: There is no one-and-done way to grow a business!

Just as you never stop learning and growing as a person, your business is never 'done.' You'll always be Creating and Sharing and Scaling Desire. You can and will continue applying the Desired Brand Effect methodology regardless of your goals, the size of your company, or the impact you want to create. As your business becomes more sophisticated or complex, you will have periods of progress and times where growth stagnates. You will always need to revisit the pillars depending on the issues you encounter in your business. It works for people at any stage in growing their brand.

So, take a look at your business now and uncover the biggest roadblock you're encountering. Are you trying to get consistent predictable sales? Are you in a place where you could use more repeat customers and less stress? Are your sales declining, or do you feel like you've lost your way? Take a look at your gaps and decide what to focus on next.. Then make sure you incorporate that into your next strategic planning and goal-setting period.

Identifying the gap is not enough on its own to make change happen. Self-awareness is key, yes, but so is strategic implementation. So, let me ask you this. How is your follow-through? If it could use a little help, this next section is going to be really important for you, especially if you have known for a while that something isn't working but you haven't been taking any action on that. In fact, I would say this next part is the most important part of the whole book, because without working on your mindset, everything we've covered is just information. The magic—and the money—is in the follow-through.

Success Mindset

Believe it or not, some of the most talented people reading this book may never end up reaching their goals. I know this is maybe a strange thing to say. However, after working with thousands of makers and creatives in my career, I notice that talent does not always translate to success. Here's why: success is an internal game, and your beliefs about yourself and your situation can be the difference between you building your dream business or not. Even if they know what to do or what they would *like* to do, they hold themselves back because they let fear run their operating system. It might also be a result of unhealed trauma, underlying beliefs from ancestors or family, or general societal beliefs. I mean, there's a reason there's a cliche called *the starving artist syndrome.* Jeff Goins says it best when he says: *real artists don't starve.*

That's why if you want to have a business, not just an expensive hobby, you need to work on your mindset daily and promote yourself to Chief Visionary Officer. A CVO understands that business is a journey of personal and professional growth. It's also an evolutionary process of your mindset and creative gifts, and when you combine that with profits and great business leadership, you are a force to be reckoned with.

Mindset work could be an entire book on its own, and we make it a core component of all of our programs because the work never ends. I can't say this enough. You always have to be working on your mindset.

There are two parts to working on your mindset:

1. Identifying the belief system that you're operating under
2. Addressing those beliefs with mindset tools

There are so many modalities you could choose to work with on your mindset, but to keep it simple, I'm going to introduce you to what I call the Rapid Reframe. Before we do that, let's take a look at some common belief systems that creatives tend to operate under. The purpose of this exercise is to self-identify if any of the beliefs are holding you back or get clarity on other beliefs that might be hindering your success so you have something to work with. You may resonate with these exact beliefs or you may find that these are not your particular limiting beliefs but that they give you some idea of what you can look for.

Identifying the belief systems that are holding you back

Being able to identify when your beliefs are getting in the way of your success is the fastest path to growth. Your beliefs can be invisible to you, like blind spots that influence the way you do something without even realizing it. We all have unconscious or subconscious biases that frame our reality. They affect our worldview and how we view ourselves. Awareness is the first step to healing any level of poor mindset or anything shaped by our belief systems that's preventing us from making progress.

Our beliefs come from our past experiences, how our parents raised us, generational trauma, and societal pressures. For example, you might have had parents who were really supportive of you being a creative child, or you might have had family members who told you that you shouldn't try to be an artist because it's hard to make money that way. Over time, with reinforcement, these stories that we were told become deep-rooted beliefs about ourselves. They run in the background and they impact our choices and the way we run our business. It also affects how successful we allow ourselves to be.

Although everyone has their own unique filters with which they view the world, in the creative world, there are some specific beliefs that are really common. These beliefs are everywhere, so I want to shine a light on the ones that I tend to find have the most negative impact on creative products business owners.

Beliefs that hold people back from running or growing a creative business include:

The 'starving artist' belief: This one comes in so many forms, but most commonly it sounds like, "I can't make money from being creative" or "I can't make money as an artist" or "I will be a sell-out if I make money from my art". I don't need to tell you that this leads creative people to stay broke instead of leaning into growing a beautiful, profitable brand based around their artistry.

The 'keep it to yourself' belief: This is the idea that creativity is limited, so you must keep what you make to yourself. If your belief sounds something like, "I can't share my ideas because people will steal my intellectual property," then you're likely to see only competition and not seek out opportunities for collaboration.

The 'making money is hard' belief: This money story is super detrimental because it can limit you no matter what direction you take your business and lead to you burning out and becoming overwhelmed. It comes from the common phrase, "Money doesn't grow on trees," but can sound like a million other stories about not being able to afford to invest, not being able to spend money, and having to conserve all your money. The flipside of this one is that money is easy to make but hard to keep. All of these come from a sense that money is a finite resource rather than a flow.

The 'creatives aren't business people' belief: Related to the starving artist belief is this idea that being creative and being a business person is mutually exclusive. Many makers perfected their craft in art school, where they learned everything to do with becoming a jeweler or a metal artist or a designer... except how to turn it into a business. As a result, many artists are equipped to do everything on the making side of their business and nothing on the sales and systems side, which is just how they like it—or so they believe until they can't make a living from doing what they love.

The 'imposter' belief: This belief often comes up when people start seeing some success and feel like they don't deserve to be where they are. At the root of this belief (and I'm going to say *all* beliefs) is the idea that we aren't good enough. If you feel like a fraud in your business, your thought patterns might go something like, "My success is a fluke" or "I did it once but I don't think I can do it again" or "people are going to find out that I don't belong here" and anything around not deserving the success that's coming your way.

Perhaps one or two of these common beliefs resonate with you. Perhaps all of them feel true for you! It's also a sure thing that you have other beliefs at play that may be getting in your way. It may also go in waves as your business evolves. Maybe you grow in your business and your confidence gets crushed because you're now playing at a different level. Maybe something happens that is new to you and you don't know how to handle the stuff that's coming your way.

DESIRED BRAND HIGHLIGHT: ALISHA MERRICK ART

The mind can be a sneaky thing and Alisha had no idea how much her negative mindset was getting in the way of her success. At one point, she didn't believe that she could be successful as an artist. She was working several part time jobs to supplement her jewelry and art business, and was often envious of other artists who were living their dreams.

One day, a friend invited her to a conference in San Francisco and, not knowing what she was getting into, Alisha agreed to go. The speaker was Abraham Hicks, the leader of the Law of Attraction movement. Throughout the event, Alisha came to a realization that her negative and resentful mindset was the reason she wasn't successful. She made a decision there and then: "If other artists can do it, so can I." That's when she started taking herself and her mindset seriously.

Alisha is a talented artist, so the moment she changed her mindset about success, things shifted fast. Since then, Alisha's business has grown from "a barely scraping by side hustle" to a full-time six-figure business with a retail store and an employee.

Mindset matters and believing that you deserve success is the most important component to being successful. You've had a glimpse of what unhelpful belief systems look like, so now let's talk about what you can do about supporting your success with a more helpful mindset.

Flipping the Script with a Rapid Reframe

In 2008 when I had to file for bankruptcy, I felt like a failure and a fraud. I doubted my place as a business owner. The recurring story I had in my head was: *I suck at business!* It wasn't until I worked on my mindset and understood that the failure of my company wasn't because of the actions I took but part of a global crisis that I was able to move forward. *Could I have done things differently to have done a better job?* Yes, and it was easier to see that within that failure there were valuable lessons to be learned.

In the context of the pandemic, we can also see how mindset was crucial to the way companies responded to world events. Some of the businesses that leaned into online sales and were unafraid to sell had record-breaking years and months. They viewed sales from a place of service.

I'm not saying that reframing your beliefs is the only thing you have to do to transform your business from one that is floundering to one that is flourishing. It's not just a matter of saying a few affirmations and all will be well. You have to take inspired action and implement all you have learned about creating a Desired Brand. However, being able to rewire your beliefs can help you feel prepared to take that necessary step and commit to that inspired action, so this is a powerful place to start.

When you realize a belief is getting in your way and you decide to do something about it, try this simple exercise to flip your beliefs:

1. Notice and note down the thought you're having.
2. Reframe the thought into something more helpful.
3. Create an affirmation for what you desire.

Let's say you want to work on the belief "it's hard to make money as an artist." Here's an example of what a rapid reframe looks like.

Notice the thought: "It's hard to make money as an artist."

Reframe the thought: "I can make money as an artist."

Create an affirmation: "I get paid exceptionally well for being creative because people value my creativity."

Here's another one that works for creatives who are undercharging for their pieces:

Notice the thought: "No one will ever pay me what this piece is really worth, because people don't have that kind of money to spend."

Reframe the thought: "There are plenty of people who value my talent and will gladly pay my prices."

Create an affirmation: "I make a good living selling my jewelry because I attract the right customers who are willing to pay me for my talent everyday."

An affirmation is simply a positive statement that reinforces the reality you want for yourself. If you haven't created one before, start by taking the belief you've flipped and thinking about the vision you hold for yourself. If affirmations don't do it for you, there are so many other modalities to address mindset issues. The rapid reframe is the simplest one for identifying your limiting beliefs and quickly turning them around, but mindset is a huge area and it's well worth exploring other options.

In our two signature programs, Laying the Foundation and Momentum, we have an abundance of in-depth mindset exercises where we dive into reframing limiting beliefs, so if you want more support with your mindset, make sure you check those out.

Where Next?

Whether you're just stepping into the role of Chief Visionary Officer of your company or are a seasoned business owner hitting the next level with your brand, mindset is the cornerstone of bringing this all together and driving forward toward your vision. Without it, you'll keep getting stuck not doing the work it takes to leap to the next level and not dealing with the growth plateaus and problems that keep coming up in your business. The difference between an overwhelmed, frustrated, burnt-out business owner and a leader who embraces support and can spend their time designing and setting the creative vision for the company is the willingness to put the pillars of the Desired Brand Effect into practice. If you're not working on your mindset and actively Creating, Sharing and Scaling Desire, you'll always struggle to create freedom with your business and the lifestyle you want it to support.

Stepping into the leading role in a successful, profitable Desired Brand starts with creating the Desired Brand Effect in your business. I've designed this method to help you attract a steady stream of the perfect customers, convert those buyers into loyal fans, and scale those results with ease. You don't have to do it alone. In fact, the more you can surround yourself with people on that same journey toward a lifestyle of freedom, financial and creative abundance, and a sense of accomplishment, the more we can all rise together. There is enough to go around for everyone to succeed.

I know you have a fire in your belly and are determined to grow. I know you won't settle for less and don't want to spend any more time stressed and cash-strapped. And I know that you are committed to your success, because you wouldn't be here if you didn't want your business to go from strength to strength. So, let me ask you this. Where do you want to be a year from now?

It's my hope and desire that you take everything you've read in this book and put it into practice. I *know* the Desired Brand Effect works because I've been where you are and I've worked with thousands of designers just like you. You can succeed, and now you have the tools to do just that. You just have to go out there and make it happen!

When you get to a place where your business is thriving and growing and you're no longer overwhelmed, your life will change. I hope this book has helped you step closer to that lifestyle of freedom, financial stability, and accomplishment that you want for yourself. If you want a bit more support to create, share and scale desire in your business, I invite you to join our coaching programs and reach that place even faster.

I'd be honored to be by your side as you grow your Desired Brand.

xo Tracy Matthews

ACKNOWLEDGEMENTS

As a little kid, I was a daydreamer. I was often misunderstood and had a difficult time focusing if I was bored or not having fun. Little did I know then how valuable daydreaming would be later in life as an entrepreneur and conscious creative. Dreaming is how I created my reality over the years. It's also how I overcame severe obstacles and hardship. If you would have told my 15 year old self that I'd be teaching jewelry makers and other handmade artists how to grow a successful business, I would have probably been intrigued but wouldn't have believed you. Yet, it was the entrepreneurial spirit that I was taught from a young age that made this journey possible (and this book a reality).

That's why I'd like to thank the people who have impacted my journey, including:

To Robin Kramer, my co-founder at Flourish & Thrive Academy. Thank you for trusting my vision and joining me for the ride to delve into the new way of "coachsulting" so many years ago.

My grandfather, Carl Karcher. You came from nothing and believed in yourself and the American Dream so much so that you built an empire from a $200 loan from Grandma. You taught me the importance of entrepreneurship, following your dreams, and aligning your business with core values. You taught so many to never stop dreaming.

My first jewelry teacher, Sue Dorman. We lost touch many years ago and you said something to me one day in class that started me on this path as a jewelry artist. Tracy, you have an eye for what the market wants. That always stuck with me and made me believe in myself.

To Phil Clements, my first consultant and business mentor. You taught me invaluable lessons that live in this book and for that I thank you. RIP.

My sister, Carlie, who believed in my dream so much that she moved to NYC to help me run my business for many years. It's been a wild ride. Thank you for the sacrifices you made to support my vision.

To the stores who took a chance on my small jewelry brand when I was starting out, including: Metier, Twist, Anthropologie, ABC Home, Bloomingdale's, the Sundance Catalog, The Claypot, and so many more.

To the many teachers, mentors, and peers who have taught me so much over the years about life and business including: Marie Forleo, Amy Porterfield, Ryan Levesque, Clint Salter, Jason R. Ayers, Margarete Nielson, Dana Obelman, Erika Lyremark, Sabina Hitchen, Laura Belgray, Susie Moore, Misty Williams, Re Perez, Selena Soo, Tracy Campoli, Taki Moore, Eric Roman, The Baby Bathwater Community, Michael Lovitch, Hollis Carter, Cathy Heller, Terri Cole, Dan Martell, Jacqueline Snyder, Michael and Amy Port, Carolyn Myss, Gino Wickman, Mark C. Winters, and Michael Gerber.

To my team, past, present, and future. Without you, none of this would have been possible. Jessica, Abie, Abby, Quay, Lisa, Shaundra, Jason,

Joseph, Ari, Sarah, Brianna, Courtney, Bean, Peter, Kris, Toby, and many more. Without you, this book wouldn't have come to life. And our coaches, Ana Maria, Nicole, Dawn, Sarah, Gwynne, Melissa, Darian, Julio, Delia, Maisha, Sabina, Karen, Andrea, Chelsea, Jessica, Inta, Kristen, Janine, and Kathy. You are the reason that we've been able to help thousands of jewelry designers, makers, retailers, and handmade artists over the years. Thank you for believing in my vision and supporting our community in the way that you do.

To the many members of our community, especially those that were brave enough to let me profile them in this book. Thank you for putting your faith and trust in me and my team to help you grow your business. You are rockstars and I'm so proud of you and all of your accomplishments for many years to come. Seeing you achieve your dreams is the reason I wake up every day!

My spiritual teachers, guides, and personal support system, including: Melanie, Anne, Barbara, Kacy, and Kim. Your support and guidance over the years has changed my life. Thank you. Thank you. Thank you.

To my soul family. Thank you for the invitation to raise our collective consciousness.

My dear friends who have believed in me and supported me during the good times and that most challenging times: Kate, Rich, Tina, Erin, Leigh, Catherine, Alex, Carrie, Re, Reed, Clint, Tracy, Laura, Susie, Danielle, Carolyn, Sabina, JJ, Erica, Shannon, Nicole, Gretchen, Georgina, Traci, Brandi, Mel, Janet, Kristi, Jonathan, Brooke, Grace, and Tina and Billy. Thank you for your friendship.

To my godparents, Jerome and Debbie and my Aunts, Barbara and Peggy. You've been like second parents to me.

My family. Mom, Dad, Beth, Michele, Jerrott, Nikki, Brad, Carlie, Christopher, and Haley. Growing up the second oldest of eight children has taught me so much about pretty much everything. Thank you for bringing your creative, light filled-children into the world.

My stepdaughters, Natalia and Tatiana. You teach me something new every day and my life is a lot more fun with you in it.

To my love, Jason R. Ayers. You are the person I'd been dreaming about for all those years and you are so worth the wait. You challenge me to be a better person. Thank you for walking into my apartment that day and looking at me all funny. More importantly, thank you for believing in me and supporting me so selflessly.

Thank *you* for reading this book. I hope that you've found at least one (and hopefully many) takeaways that you can implement into your business. I wish you every success you desire.

xo, Tracy

RESOURCES

Here are some of my favorite books, tools, websites and programs that I've mentioned through the book and love to recommend. You can access these directly at DesiredBrandEffect.com/resources along with more exclusive content.

CHAPTER 1: BECOMING THE CHIEF VISIONARY OFFICER OF YOUR BUSINESS

Books

Gerber, M.E., The E-Myth, (1995), HarperCollins Publishers Inc

CHAPTER 3: YOUR BRAND ASSETS

Books

Perez, R., Your Brand Should Be Gay (Even If You're Not): The Art and Science of Creating an Authentic Brand, (2020), Lioncrest Publishing

Websites

1000 True Fans article: flourishthriveacademy.com/truefans

StrongBrands website: timcalkins.com

Shopify: flourishthriveacademy.com/shopify

Resources by Flourish & Thrive Academy

Pricing and Brand Assets: DesiredBrandEffect.com/resources

Brands mentioned

Jennifer Dawes: dawes-design.com

Dana Kellin: danakellin.com

Melissa Joy Manning: melissajoymanning.com

Chan Luu: chanluu.com

viv&ingrid: shopvivandingrid.com

Alex Camacho: acidqueenjewelry.com

Jamie Joseph: jamiejoseph.com

Lorraine West: lorrainewestjewelry.com

Twyla Dill: twyladill.com

Cathy Waterman: cathywaterman.com

Meghan Patrice Riley: meghanpatriceriley.com

Nicole Gariepy: fantaseajewelry.com

Allyson Hayes: preciouselementsdesigns.com

CHAPTER 4: YOUR AUDIENCE

Resources by Flourish & Thrive Academy
Dream Client Clarity Kit: flourishthriveacademy.com/dcck

CHAPTER 5: YOUR BRAND VOICE

Books

Miller, D., Building a StoryBrand, (2017), HarperCollins Leadership

Sinek, S., Start With Why, (2009), Portfolio

Websites

Start With Why: flourishthriveacademy.com/startwithwhy

CHAPTER 6: MARKETING

Books

Vaynerchuk, G., Jab, Jab, Jab, Right Hook, (2013), HarperCollins US

Websites

Shopify: flourishthriveacademy.com/shopify

Resources by Flourish & Thrive Academy

Thrive by Design podcast Lisa Lehman episode: flourishthriveacademy
.com/121

Thrive by Design podcast Sarah DeAngelo episode: flourishthrive
academy.com/98

Thrive by Design podcast Jeana and Jared Rushton episode:
flourishthriveacademy.com/178

Sample marketing plan calendar: DesiredBrandEffect.com/resources

Content marketing ideas: DesiredBrandEffect.com/resources

Automated email sequences resource: DesiredBrandEffect
.com/resources

Virtual Trunk Shows that Sell: flourishthriveacademy.com/vts

Turning One Piece of Content into 35: DesiredBrandEffect.com/resources

CHAPTER 7: SALES

Books

Goins, J., Real Artists Don't Starve: Timeless Strategies for Thriving in the New Creative Age, (2017), HarperCollins Leadership

Pink, D.H., To Sell Is Human, (2013), Riverhead Books

Websites

Robin Kramer: RedBootConsulting.com

Shopify: flourishthriveacademy.com/shopify

StreamYard: flourishthriveacademy.com/streamyard

CommentSold: flourishthriveacademy.com/commentsold

Power Poses: flourishthriveacademy.com/amycuddy

CHAPTER 8: EXCEPTIONAL SERVICE

Websites

Insightly: insightly.com

HubSpot: hubspot.com

CHAPTER 10: STRATEGIC BUSINESS PLANNING

Books

Herold, C., Vivid Vision, (2018), Lioncrest Publishing

Horan, J., The One-Page Business Plan for the Creative Entrepreneur, (2015), The One Page Business Plan Company

CHAPTER 11: SYSTEMS AND AUTOMATION

Websites

DesiredBrandEffect.com/resources

Klaviyo: flourishthriveacademy.com/klaviyo

Omnisend: flourishthriveacademy.com/omnisend

Insightly: insightly.com

HubSpot: hubspot.com

Quickbooks: quickbooks.com

Xero: xero.com

Loom: loom.com

Screencastify: screencastify.com

Screenflow: telestream.net

Otter: otter.ai

Scribie: scribie.com

Rev: rev.com

Process Street: process.st

Google Drive: drive.google.com

Dropbox: dropbox.com

Asana: asana.com

Trello: trello.com

Lastpass: lastpass.com

Pipedrive: pipedrive.com

Zendesk: zendesk.com

Contactually: contactually.com

Zoho: zoho.com

CHAPTER 12: GETTING THE RIGHT SUPPORT

Resources by Flourish & Thrive Academy

Thrive by Design podcast Twyla Dill episode: flourishthriveacademy .com/twyla

CHAPTER 13: MAKING THE DESIRED BRAND EFFECT WORK FOR YOU

Books

Goins, J., Real Artists Don't Starve: Timeless Strategies for Thriving in the New Creative Age, (2017), HarperCollins Leadership

FIND OUT MORE ABOUT OUR SIGNATURE PROGRAMS

Laying the Foundation: flourishthriveacademy.com/ltf

Momentum: flourishthriveacademy.com/momentum

ELSEWHERE ON THE INTERNET

Podcast: flourishthriveacademy.com/podcast

Facebook: facebook.com/FlourishThriveAcademy

Instagram: instagram.com/flourish_thrive

YouTube: youtube.com/FlourishThriveAcademy

Pinterest: pinterest.com/flourishthrive

Opt-in to the Desired Brand Effect and other masterclass trainings: DesiredBrandEffect.com/resources

ABOUT THE AUTHOR
TRACY MATTHEWS

Tracy Matthews started designing jewelry as a teenager. Her first pieces were wire-wrapped pearls with materials purchased at the Bead Shop in Laguna Beach, California. She officially found her passion for jewelry at Loyola Marymount University when she had the opportunity to take a jewelry-making class as an elective. Her professor, Sue Dorman, planted a seed during that class and inspired her to pursue her passion for jewelry design.

Throughout university, Matthews worked in boutiques right around the time when the independent jewelry scene started booming. Seeing the cool jewelry designers like Erica Courtney and Bettina Duncan inspired her to start selling her jewelry on the side. She learned the art of selling as a sales associate at Nordstrom where she continued working until she turned her side-hustle into a full-time business. In 1998, she launched Tracy Matthews Designs, Inc. and sold her jewelry first in local stores and eventually internationally around the world.

Her designs have been sold in over 350 stores around the world including the Sundance Catalog, Anthropologie, Bloomingdale's, ABC Home, Twist, and Metier. Notable media placements include Elle, InStyle, Us Weekly, Real Simple, Martha Stewart Weddings, Entrepreneur, and the Today Show. She's been interviewed on countless podcasts and programs including Yahoo! Finance, American Fashion Podcast, Online Marketing Made Easy, EOFire, and Creative Live. Fun fact: Revlon commissioned her to make a 20-year commemorative piece for Halle Berry.

In 2008, the Global Financial Crisis wiped out her first company. As bankruptcy notices started rolling in from her key accounts, she was left with a difficult question: what next? Through some soul searching, Matthews decided to close her first company to start a new business model designed around the lifestyle she desired. She was exhausted and reinvented her business to become a private jeweler based in NYC. Using The Desired Brand Effect, she was able to scale her company quickly to have her most personally profitable month within 18 months of filing for bankruptcy.

The Desired Brand Effect was the system she developed to position, grow and scale four companies across multiple industries including jewelry, education, and branding. She's made it her mission to make building a business fun and joyful and that's why she loves helping others.

Spirituality, consciousness, mindset and yoga have been pivotal in shaping the way she teaches business. Right around the time she started her first business, she started teaching yoga in San Francisco and then NYC. She brought a real-life quality into her classes by understanding the pressures of entrepreneurship, business, and city life.. That's why mindset has become such a powerful force in her success and the success of her students.

Matthews co-founded Flourish & Thrive Academy with her friend Robin Kramer in 2012. Their goal was to bust the norms of the tight-lipped jewelry industry and create a community where the makers actually shared their secrets to support each other. As the industry started evolving and online sales became a serious consideration for the future of the industry, Matthews and Kramer moved on in their own direction. Matthews runs Flourish & Thrive Academy and Kramer has coaching programs for designers who sell wholesale at Redboot Consulting.

Today, Flourish & Thrive's signature programs include Laying the Foundation, Momentum Coaching and the Train Your Customers to Buy From You online workshop. Matthews hosts a weekly podcast called Thrive by Design where she interviews leaders in the industry and shares business advice, marketing tips, and general inspiration. She is also the founder of the #creativesruletheworld movement. It's her belief that creativity is the most valuable asset in business—it's how great brands are formed, problems are solved, and people live happier lives.

She lives in Arizona with her partner Jason and his two daughters. She considers NYC her second home, loves to travel, and is the proud auntie to 23 nieces and nephews.

Made in the USA
Las Vegas, NV
09 November 2021